It's another Quality Book from CGP

This book is for 11-14 year olds.

Whatever subject you're doing it's the same
old story — there are lots of facts and you've just got
to learn them. KS3 English is no different.

Happily this CGP book gives you all that important
information as clearly and concisely as possible.

It's also got some daft bits in to try and make the whole
experience at least vaguely entertaining for you.

What CGP is all about

Our sole aim here at CGP is to produce the highest quality
books — carefully written, immaculately presented and
dangerously close to being funny.

Then we work our socks off to get them out to you
— at the cheapest possible prices.

MACBETH — TRAGIC COMICS

Contents

SECTION 5 — THE SET SCENES

SECTION 6 — WRITING AN ESSAY

SECTION 7 — TYPES OF QUESTIONS

Published by Coordination Group Publications Ltd.

Contributors:

Angela Billington
Chris Dennett
Bill Shakespeare
Katherine Stewart
Tim Wakeling
James Paul Wallis
Andrew Wright

and:
Tim Major
Claire Thompson

ISBN   1 84146 148 2

Groovy website: www.cgpbooks.co.uk

Jolly bits of clipart from CorelDRAW

Printed by Elanders Hindson, Newcastle upon Tyne.

Preparing Your Answer

Preparation — sounds like a lot of work but it'll make the exam loads easier. Work out exactly what you've got to do before you start writing. It's the only way to get good marks.

Read Through the Scenes Again

You should know your set scenes pretty darn well by the time you sit the SAT. But, even if you know them backwards you need to read them through again when you get into the test.

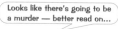
Looks like there's going to be a murder — better read on...

Go through each passage quickly, looking at who is in the scene and what happens. Jot these things down — it'll help you clear your head.

Then read through the whole thing carefully. If you don't understand a few lines, keep going — come back to them later.

Plan Your Answer

When you're feeling panicky at the start of an exam planning seems like a waste of time. Well it's not a waste of time. You've got to do it or your answer will be a pile of pants.

e.g. Q. How does Macbeth persuade himself to murder Duncan, and how does Lady Macbeth help to persuade him?

1) First, go through the extracts and underline anything the characters say that helps answer the question. For this question you'd best concentrate on what Macbeth and Lady Macbeth say.

2) Now, write down what the main parts of your essay are going to be —

   • what Macbeth says about NOT WANTING to kill Duncan
   • what Macbeth decides when he's on his own
   • how Macbeth reacts when Lady Macbeth tries to persuade him
   • language Lady Macbeth uses to try and persuade Macbeth to change his mind

3) Make sure you use all these points in your essay.

Some Questions are Really Two in Disguise

Keep an eye out for tasks that ask you to do more than one thing. These are really two questions in one.

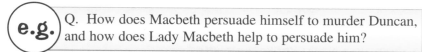
Q. What does Macbeth's reaction to the news of his wife's death tell you about their relationship and how much more does he seem concerned by the news of Birnam Wood moving?

Here's one question — it's about the relationship of Macbeth and Lady Macbeth.

... And here's another — how does this compare with his concern at Birnam Wood moving?

I'm singin' in the rain...

Two things at once...

If you choose a task like this, be bloomin' sure you do both parts of it.

Tango for beginners — one step at a time...

They look scary, but these questions aren't bad if you follow these steps. Read through the passage first, make notes on what happens, and make a plan. Do all that and you'll do tons better...

Writing Well & Giving Examples

Three more <u>key things</u> you have to do here — make sure you get them <u>clear</u> in your head now.

You've Got to *Write Properly*

Stuff this for a game of skittles — I'm off to England.

1) You've got to keep your <u>spelling</u> and <u>punctuation</u> top notch or you'll be making your writing harder to read and chucking marks down the pan.

2) Write in <u>paragraphs</u>. Every time you want to talk about a <u>new idea</u>, start a <u>new paragraph</u>.

3) Here's the tough one — you've got to try to sound <u>interested</u> in the play, even if you don't like it. Use loads of <u>interesting</u> <u>words</u> and <u>phrases</u>, like this:

Shakespeare makes your spine tingle with excitement in this scene — right from the start you know that it's going to end in a fight.

Give *Loads* of *Examples* **and** *Quotes*

They want you to give <u>examples</u> from the scene that have <u>something to do</u> with the task you chose. That includes using <u>quotes</u> — these will convince them you <u>really know</u> your stuff.

Why didn't I read Macbeth?

Make sure you stick your quotes in <u>speech marks</u> and only use the <u>exact words</u> that Shakespeare uses.

You also need to <u>explain why</u> each bit is <u>relevant</u> — <u>how</u> it helps <u>answer</u> the question.

You won't get <u>high marks</u> for what you write unless you give <u>examples</u> to back it up.

Write About Any *Versions* of the Play You've *Seen*

In your answer, you can write about <u>any version</u> of the play you've seen, as long as it's <u>relevant</u> to the task. That includes any <u>videos</u>, <u>films</u> or <u>theatre productions</u> you've seen.

Aaargh!

Die!

Just remember, <u>each</u> version can be very <u>different</u>. The <u>director</u> can change the <u>costumes</u>, the <u>setting</u> or the <u>personalities</u> of the <u>characters</u>.

It's a good idea to mention these things. Just make sure you say <u>which</u> version you're talking about.

In the 1937 film of the play the director, Tintin Quarantino, used loud music and big explosions to show that Shakespeare is really exciting.

Hatred of jewels? — no, a version to treasure...

Look into my eyes... you are feeling very sleepy... everything I say you will remember... In your SAT you will back up every point with a quote... In your SAT you will back up every point with a quote...

Stage Directions, Acts and Scenes

Loads of things may seem <u>strange</u> when you first read Shakespeare, but you have to understand them for the exam. It's <u>mega important</u> to learn these special play terms — so <u>get to it</u>.

Stage Directions <u>Explain the</u> Action

<u>Stage directions</u> show the actors <u>what</u> to do, <u>when</u> to come in and when to <u>leave</u> the stage. They are little phrases, usually written in brackets, or at least in italics.

> **This is a stage direction telling you Banquo and his son Fleance are attacked by murderers.**

[*The first Murderer strikes out the light while the others assault Banquo.*]

BANQUO   O, treachery! Fly, good Fleance, fly, fly, fly!
             Thou may'st revenge — O slave!

> **Another stage direction. Banquo is killed. Fleance makes a fast exit from the stage.**

[*Dies. Fleance escapes.*]

> **The <u>character names</u> here tell you who's <u>speaking</u>. So it's Banquo saying these lines.**

3 MURDERER   Who did strike out the light?
1 MURDERER   Was't not the way?
3 MURDERER   There's but one down: the son is fled.
2 MURDERER   We have lost
Best half of our affair.
1 MURDERER   Well let's away,
And say how much is done.
                             [*Exeunt*]

Act 3, Scene 3, 19-25

> **Exeunt is a daft word. All it means is that more than one person <u>leaves</u> the stage. At the <u>end</u> of a scene it means <u>everyone leaves</u>.**

Could I have you murderers centre stage now please...

STAGE DIRECTING

> Remember that a <u>play</u> is meant to be <u>performed not read</u>. So <u>read the stage directions</u> because they're <u>dead handy</u> for <u>imagining</u> what the play would <u>look like</u>.

Acts <u>and</u> Scenes Divide up <u>the Play</u>

1) The play is divided into <u>five</u> big sections called <u>acts</u>. Each act is like an <u>episode</u> of a TV serial — loads of things happen in it, but it's only a <u>part of the whole thing</u>.

2) Each act is made up of <u>smaller</u> sections called <u>scenes</u>. A scene shows you a <u>small bit</u> of the story. Then a new scene starts and shows you the next bit. <u>Easy</u>.

3) Scenes are a way of <u>breaking up</u> the story. They <u>change</u> if <u>time has passed</u> or if the action is <u>moving to somewhere else</u>. One scene could be set in the evening and the next one the following day. Or a scene could take place in <u>Macbeth's castle</u> and the next out in the <u>fields of Scotland</u>.

<u>Unlike children, plays should be scene and heard...</u>

OK, some little things to help you really <u>get to grips</u> with plays. Acts and scenes <u>break up the action</u> into easily digestible little <u>bite-sized</u> pieces. Stage directions tell you who's doing what and how, so you can <u>imagine</u> what the play would look like — cool, huh...

Macbeth as a Play

More <u>hints</u> to help you understand Shakespeare's plays — <u>get learning</u>.

Macbeth is Meant to be <u>Watched</u> <u>not</u> <u>Read</u>

What a weirdo!

Let me SHOW you the art of true magic —come close and marvel at my STORY...

1) *Macbeth* is a play, not a book. There is a <u>massive, huge</u> <u>difference</u> between a Shakespeare play and a novel or short story. A novel tells a story by <u>describing</u> it to you. A play tells a story by <u>showing</u> it to you.

2) When you read it, all you get is what the characters <u>say</u>. It's often pretty hard to <u>follow</u> what's going on.

3) You've got to try to <u>imagine</u> what's happening. Think about what the people are <u>like</u>, and how you think they would <u>speak</u> and <u>act</u>.

4) If you can, watch a <u>film</u> or <u>TV version</u> of the play. It's a great way to bring it to life — and you're allowed to <u>write about it</u> in your SAT, as long as it <u>fits in</u> with the question. Just <u>remember</u> <u>every version</u> of the play will be <u>different</u> so always <u>explain which one</u> you are talking about.

Sometimes Characters <u>Talk</u> <u>to</u> <u>Themselves</u>

This seems <u>strange</u>. People in real life don't <u>usually</u> talk to themselves — if they did, pretty soon you'd start to <u>worry</u> about them.

Characters in plays do this so the audience can hear what they're <u>thinking</u> and <u>feeling</u>. They're really talking for the <u>benefit</u> of the audience.

Did you know talking to yourself is one of the first signs of madness?

Don't be ridiculous — what rot and nonsense!

Sometimes characters speak thoughts <u>aloud</u> when <u>other</u> characters are on the stage. When you see the word [Aside], that's what's happening — the <u>audience</u> can hear, but the <u>other</u> characters can't.

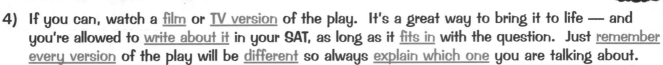

MACBETH Go bid thy mistress, when my drink is ready,
        She strike upon the bell. Get thee to bed.
[EXIT SERVANT]   Is this a dagger which I see before me,
        The handle toward my hand? Come let me clutch thee: —
        I have thee not, and yet I see thee still.

                     Act 2, Scene 1, lines 31-35

Macbeth's dreaming the dagger — that's why he can't pick it up when he tries to.

The servant has gone. Macbeth is on his own.

Macbeth is <u>thinking</u> these things and <u>saying them to himself</u>. People don't usually think out loud, but you wouldn't know what was going on in Macbeth's head if he didn't <u>tell</u> you. Shakespeare makes him say it <u>out loud</u>.

Axe-shun — avoiding hatchets?...

Use your <u>imagination</u> as much as possible and <u>never ever forget</u> that it's not just a book. Remember characters <u>think out loud</u> — which is a bit <u>bizarre</u>. When there's an [aside] before an actor speaks, nobody on stage can hear what they're saying — a bit weird, but <u>pretty groovy</u>...

Odd Language

Blimey — this complicated language can be confusing.
There are certain ways of reading it so it makes more sense — check 'em out...

Don't Stop Reading at the End of Each Line

Here's a simple point — but it's one you mustn't ever forget.

1) Even though each line starts with a capital letter, it doesn't mean it's a separate sentence. Just ignore the capitals and follow the punctuation.

> Are ye fantastical, or that indeed
> Which outwardly ye show?
>
> Act 1, Scene 3, 51-2

2) There's no full stop here so carry on to the next line.

3) There isn't a break in the sentence even when it moves to the next line. You've got to read it as if it's written like this:

> Are ye fantastical, or that indeed which outwardly ye show?

Follow the punctuation, not the lines — or none of it will make sense.

Look Out for Words in a Funny Order

Another nasty reason it can be so tricky to understand Shakespeare is because he wrote loads of really complicated long sentences. You're gonna have to monkey around with the word order to get it to make sense before you tackle the language itself.

1) Here's a typical sentence — it looks really complicated.

> When in swinish sleep
> Their drenched natures lie, as in death,
> What cannot you and I perform upon
> Th'unguarded Duncan?
>
> Act 1, Scene 7, 67-70

2) It's hard because the words are in a funny order. The whole sentence is back-to-front — we can switch the order around to make it easier to understand.

> What cannot you and I perform upon th'unguarded Duncan when their drenched natures lie in swinish sleep as in death?

This basically means: we can do whatever we want to Duncan when his guards are drunk.

Hiccup!

Your words have been proven to be drunken and disorderly. There is nothing humorous or funny about such word order — and I shall be handing out long sentences to one and all...

Weird, lanky, crone — odd long-witch...

Just two things to weld into your head. Don't stop reading at the end of a line, wait for the full stop — and try to play around with the word order in long sentences so that they make more sense. That's it for this page — easy-peasy lemon squeezy...

More Odd Language

You may be <u>confused</u> at first by the <u>old words</u> Shakespeare uses. Here's a <u>guide</u> to the most <u>common</u> ones and what they <u>mean</u>. After a while, they won't seem so <u>strange</u>...

Watch Out for Old Words — Mind Your Thees & Thous

These <u>three words</u> turn up all the time —
they make sentences <u>look</u> much <u>harder</u> than they really are.

Thou = You   **Thee = You**   **Thy = Your**

> Whence cam'st thou, worthy Thane?
> *Act 1, Scene 2, 48*

> So well thy words become thee, as thy wounds:
> They smack of honour both.
> *Act 1, Scene 2, 43-44*

They're just an <u>old way</u> of saying <u>you</u> and <u>your</u>.

Verbs can be Different Too

How to look harder than you really are...

wert thou = were you

thou wilt = you will

See thee — I'll have thee I will! I'm well hard — thou'll not stand a chance.

thou hast = you have

thou swear'st = you swear

> This can seem <u>difficult</u>, but really it isn't. <u>Take the 't' off</u> the end of the <u>verb</u> and you'll be able to <u>figure out</u> what it <u>means</u>.

Here are Some Common Old Words

1) hence = from here

> Help me hence, ho!
> *Act 2, Scene 3, 111*

2) ere = before

> That will be ere the set of sun.
> *Act 1, Scene 1, 5*

"<u>Whence</u>" means "from where" and "<u>thence</u>" means "from there".

"<u>Hie</u>" means "<u>go</u>"
"<u>Murther</u>" means "<u>murder</u>"
"<u>hither</u>" means "<u>to here</u>"

3) wherefore = for what reason/why

> Wherefore did you so?
> *Act 2, Scene 3, 100*

It means "<u>why</u> did you do it" — not "where".

Get thee hence — chicks won't do...

Because it was written ages ago *Macbeth* is <u>choccer-full</u> of strange old words — don't let 'em faze you.

Poetry

Shakespeare wrote <u>mostly</u> in <u>poetry</u> — a lot of the <u>strange things</u> he does with words and sentences are <u>to fit the rules</u> of poetry. <u>It figures</u> that if you <u>understand</u> a bit about how poetry <u>should be written</u>, the play will make <u>more sense</u>. But <u>don't worry</u> — you <u>don't</u> have to talk about poetry in the exam.

Rules of Poetry

Practically all of <u>*Macbeth*</u> is written in poetry — a tiny bit is in prose.
<u>Prose</u> is any kind of language that <u>isn't poetry</u>.

Lawks — what an absolutely capital letter! Oh, I say. What a top-notch way to start — sheer poetry.

You Know it's Poetry when...

— every line starts with a <u>capital letter</u>
<u>AND</u>
— every line has <u>10-11 syllables</u>

But not every line has to rhyme.

Except when the <u>witches</u> speak.

Shakespeare Fiddles Things Around to Make Them Fit

One of the things which makes Shakespeare <u>pretty tricky</u> to read is that he <u>fiddles with the words</u> to make most of the lines have 10 or 11 syllables. He also <u>jiggles sentences</u> to make shorter ones <u>fit the pattern</u> of the poetry.

① He often <u>runs two words together</u> and misses letters out.

Hark!
Who lies i'th'second chamber?
Act 2, Scene 2, 21

"i'th'" means "in the"

② In <u>conversation</u> Shakespeare <u>sometimes splits</u> the syllables between <u>two or more</u> lines — so these lines <u>add up</u> to 10 or 11 syllables <u>together</u>. That's why they're <u>staggered</u> to show that they <u>are all</u> part of <u>one line of poetry</u>.

Lady Macbeth Did not you speak?
Macbeth   When?
Lady Macbeth   Now.
Macbeth   As I descended?
Act 2, Scene 2, 16-19

A sonnet in a marathon — poetry in motion...

Remember that Shakespeare wrote in poetry — it'll seem <u>pretty darned confusing</u> if you forget. All these rules about poetry are just there <u>to help you</u> understand the play better — you don't need to write about them in the exam. Phew, what a relief...

Revision Summary

There's a fair bit to take in here to understand the play. But it's all pretty vital — you have to understand the scene to answer questions well on it. I know the poetry stuff can seem tricky, but it's only there to help you understand everything better. Right — get your teeth into these questions...

1) Why are stage directions mega handy?   a) they help you find the stage   b) they tell the stage where to go   c) they help you imagine what the play would look like

2) What does "[Exeunt]" mean?

3) What are bigger, acts or scenes?

4) How many acts are there?   a) 3.5   b) 5   c) 12

5) What's the difference between the way a novel tells a story and the way a play does?

6) Why do characters in plays talk to themselves?   a) because they're stark raving bonkers   b) because nobody else will listen   c) to let the audience know what they are thinking or feeling

7) What word is used in stage directions to show that the character is speaking so that nobody else on the stage can hear them?

8) Should you always stop reading at the end of each line?

9) Why? / Why not?

10) Does a capital letter always mean a new sentence is starting?

11) Why/why not?

12) One crafty thing Shakespeare did was to write: a) long and complicated sentences   b) shopping lists for his wife   c) e-mails to his friends

13) What do you need to monkey around with before you try to work out the meaning of long sentences?

14) What do "thou" and "thee" mean?

15) What does "wherefore" mean?   a) where   b) why   c) what

16) What does "murther" mean?

17) What does "ere" mean?   a) here   b) ear   c) before

18) What two things does Shakespeare do to make the lines fit a pattern?

I SAID "UNDERSTAND" __NOT__ "STAND UNDER" THE PLAY   — JEESCH..!

Who's Who in the Play

Och aye... the main characters have all got <u>Scottish</u> names. Here's a <u>quick guide</u> to them.

The Big Two — the Macbeths

Macbeth

"I'm so important I had a play named after me."

Lady Macbeth

These two are the <u>most important</u> characters in the play.

King Duncan and his Two Kids

Duncan

Donalbain

Malcolm

Duncan is King at the <u>start</u>. His son <u>Malcolm</u> gets to be King at the <u>end</u>. The other son, Donalbain, isn't in it much.

Hecate and the Three Witches

Three Witches

Hecate

Gross, eh? But they can <u>predict the future</u>.

Banquo and Son

Banquo

Fleance

Banquo's a <u>nobleman</u>. Macbeth has him <u>killed</u>. His son, Fleance, <u>escapes</u>.

The Macduffs

Son

Macduff

Lady Macduff

Macbeth has Macduff's <u>family</u> killed. Then <u>Macduff</u> kills Macbeth. Got it?

More Noblemen

There's a bunch of other characters, mostly <u>Scottish noblemen</u>. Don't worry about them too much.

Thistle test you — learn those Scottish names...

Okay, so they're <u>not</u> the kind of names you hear every day. Tough — that's what people were called in the <u>11th century</u> in <u>Scotland</u>. Use this page to learn <u>who's who</u>. It'll really help.

Macbeth

Macbeth's the <u>main character</u>. Not surprising, really, given what the play's called. It's a pretty <u>good bet</u> your SAT will ask you <u>something</u> about him — so you have to know <u>what he's like</u>.

He's a Brave Hero — and a Brutal Murderer

1) The first thing we hear about Macbeth is what a <u>brave warrior</u> he is (Act 1 Scene 2). And he dies bravely too — he <u>fights</u> to the last even though he knows he's doomed (Act 5 Scene 8).

I'm not sure about this...

Ah, go on, go on, go on... You will, you will, you will, you will, you will, you will...

2) But he's also a <u>cold and calculating killer</u>. In Act 2 Scene 2 he murders Duncan because he wants to be King. And he has Macduff's family and Banquo <u>killed</u>.

3) Some people think Macbeth must be <u>evil</u> because of all the terrible crimes he commits. Others think he's not so bad really — maybe he kills Duncan because he's very <u>ambitious</u> and he's <u>egged on</u> by his missus. And he kills Macduff's family and Banquo out of <u>fear</u> of losing his position.

He Struggles With His Conscience

1) Macbeth knows that killing Duncan is <u>wrong</u>. He decides not to do it in Act 1 Scene 7 — but Lady Macbeth talks him into it. He feels bad about it beforehand, and really <u>guilty</u> afterwards.

Quit buggin' me, will ya?

2) In Act 3, when he has had Banquo killed, he's reduced to a <u>guilty wreck</u> when Banquo's <u>ghost</u> appears. But by Act 5, when he hears about Lady Macbeth's death, he seems <u>world-weary</u> and <u>cynical</u>.

3) Macbeth wants to be <u>manly</u>. Lady Macbeth persuades him to kill Duncan by calling him a <u>coward</u>. But if he was truly brave, he'd have stood up for what he knew was the <u>right thing to do</u>.

He's Influenced by the Supernatural

1) The <u>supernatural</u> stuff in this play affects Macbeth the most. He sees a <u>dagger</u> when he's going to kill Duncan. And he's the <u>only one</u> who can see <u>Banquo's ghost</u>. These might be <u>supernatural events</u> or just <u>Macbeth's imagination</u> — but it's still weird stuff.

2) At first Macbeth is <u>sceptical</u> about the Witches. When he's made Thane of Cawdor he <u>starts to believe</u> them. But he still thinks he can <u>alter their prophecies</u>. By the end Macbeth completely trusts their predictions. When they don't happen in quite the way he'd like, he falls to pieces.

Macbeth — more like Macdeath if you ask me...

Shakespeare <u>deliberately</u> made Macbeth so <u>complicated</u> to make the play <u>interesting</u>.
It's because he's such a <u>brave hero</u> at the start that it's such a <u>tragedy</u> when he does become evil.

Lady Macbeth

Lady Macbeth is the other <u>really big character</u> in the play. Just like Macbeth, she's a pretty <u>complicated</u> character too. But if you get to know <u>what she's like</u>, you'll be fine in your SAT.

She's <u>Cold</u>, <u>Nasty</u> and <u>Hard As Nails</u>

1) In Act 1 Lady Macbeth is very <u>scary</u> indeed. She's just as <u>ambitious</u> as Macbeth — when she gets his letter, she <u>immediately</u> assumes that they need to kill Duncan. She's much more <u>ruthless</u> than her husband.

2) She knows <u>exactly what she's doing</u>, and she knows no <u>normal woman</u> would plan this murder. That's why she <u>appeals</u> to the spirit world to "<u>unsex</u>" her and fill her full of "<u>direst cruelty</u>".

Help! Get me outta here...

3) Macbeth has doubts about killing Duncan and Lady Macbeth <u>persuades</u> him to go through with it. She tells him he's a coward and says she would <u>kill her own baby</u> if she'd sworn to do it, like Macbeth had sworn to kill Duncan.

4) But she does have a <u>softer side</u> too. She says she knows how "<u>tender</u>" it is to <u>nurse a baby</u>. And she says she <u>couldn't kill</u> Duncan herself because he <u>reminded her</u> of her <u>father</u>. These show that she is at least <u>capable</u> of feeling <u>love and affection</u>.

She's <u>Clever</u> and <u>Quick-Witted</u>

1) She comes up with the <u>cunning plot</u> to drug Duncan's servants and <u>frame</u> them for the murder.

2) When Duncan's murder is discovered, Lady Macbeth <u>pretends to faint</u>. This cleverly <u>draws attention</u> away from the not-very-convincing speech that Macbeth is making.

3) And when Macbeth is <u>acting oddly</u> because he's terrified by Banquo's ghost, Lady Macbeth <u>covers up</u> for him before he says something that gives the game away.

She Goes <u>Mad With Guilt</u> and <u>Kills Herself</u>

ACE SOAP
Removes the most stubborn guilty feelings

SOAP

1) Early in the play, Lady Macbeth is the <u>strong one</u> while Macbeth struggles with his guilty conscience. But she is only <u>repressing</u> her guilty feelings. When her conscience catches up with her, she can't cope with it and she goes <u>totally mad</u> with <u>guilt</u>.

2) She keeps <u>washing her hands</u> — in the hope that she can <u>wash away</u> her feelings of guilt just as easily as the <u>blood</u> after Duncan's murder. In the end, guilt drives her so mad that she <u>kills herself</u>.

Always washing — more like Lady Macbath...

Phew, there's a <u>lot to learn</u> about Lady Macbeth. But it's <u>worth doing</u> because she and Macbeth are the <u>most important</u> characters by miles. All the rest are much <u>simpler</u> to understand.

Banquo, Duncan and Malcolm

Okay, we've got the main two characters out of the way. But you still need to know about these other guys — there's a good chance you'll get at least one of them in your SAT.

Banquo's a *Nice Guy... Or Is He?*

1) Banquo is a brave nobleman. He is praised for his courage in battle — just like Macbeth. And Macbeth even goes on about how inferior he feels in comparison to Banquo, because Banquo's such a great guy — he's so wise and fearless.

2) Banquo is quite calm and not bothered when he meets the Witches. When Macbeth wants to talk about the Witches' prophecies, Banquo says fine — as long as Macbeth doesn't want him to do anything dishonourable.

CRIMESTOPPERS

Do you know who killed this man?
Call Fife 1212 now

3) But it's not all sweetness and light. After all, Banquo suspects Macbeth murdered Duncan — yet he doesn't do anything about it. Maybe he's slyly ambitious — after all, the Witches did say that his descendants would be Kings one day.

4) Because of what the Witches said, Macbeth thinks Banquo and his son are a threat to him, so he gets hired killers to murder them. Banquo is killed but his son, Fleance, escapes. Banquo's ghost comes back to haunt Macbeth.

Duncan's *Good, but Too Trusting*

1) Duncan's the King at the start of the play. He's a kind and generous man — he hands out honours to Macbeth and Malcolm, and gives Lady Macbeth a diamond. Everyone thinks Duncan's a great guy — even Macbeth, the man who murders him.

You're not going to murder me, are you?

No, no.

2) Duncan's downfall is that he's too trusting. He never thinks it might be a bad idea to stay at Macbeth's place.

Malcolm's a *Bit More Shrewd* than his Dad

I'm evil, me... only kidding.

1) Malcolm lives in England while Macbeth is ruling Scotland. He's learnt a lesson from his dad's murder. When Macduff comes to see him he shrewdly tests Macduff's loyalty by pretending to be a bad guy, when he's actually whiter than white.

2) Malcolm goes to Scotland with an army. He proves he's clever by coming up with the plan to disguise the soldiers with branches. Malcolm becomes King of Scotland when they win. He shows he's generous — by making all the Thanes into Earls.

Banquo was brave — dead brave...

These characters all have really important roles in the play. All three of them are such good guys that they are a great contrast to nasty old Macbeth. Make sure you know how they all fit in.

The Macduffs and the Weird Sisters

Macbeth, Lady Macbeth, Banquo, Duncan, Malcolm... <u>not many more</u> characters to go now. Once you've done this page you'll know about <u>everyone</u> but the piddly little <u>minor</u> characters.

Macduff is <u>Honest</u> and <u>True</u>

1) Macduff's a <u>nobleman</u>, like Macbeth. He's a <u>straight-up</u>, <u>decent</u> kind of guy — his honour contrasts with Macbeth. He discovers Duncan's murder, and he's <u>genuinely horrified</u> by it.

2) Macduff goes to England to tell Malcolm what a <u>terrible state</u> Scotland is in, and to ask for Malcolm's <u>help</u> in fighting Macbeth. Malcolm tests Macduff's loyalty by pretending to be a <u>bad man</u> — and Macduff proves he's <u>honest</u> by saying that if Malcolm really is that bad, he <u>doesn't deserve to live</u>, let alone to rule Scotland.

3) But Macduff makes a <u>major mistake</u> by going to England and leaving his wife and kids behind. When he <u>finds out</u> Macbeth has had them murdered, he is stricken with <u>grief</u>. He gets his <u>revenge</u> on Macbeth by <u>killing him</u> in battle.

I'm sure I've forgotten something...

4) We see <u>Lady Macduff</u> and one of the Macduff <u>children</u> only when they are <u>gruesomely murdered</u>. They are both sweet and <u>sympathetic</u> characters. Nice Lady Macduff is a <u>contrast</u> to nasty horrible Lady Macbeth.

The <u>Weird Sisters</u> are...<u>Weird</u>

1) The <u>Weird Sisters</u> are also called the <u>Three Witches</u>. They are <u>supernatural</u>. They look like <u>hideous women with beards</u>, and Macbeth and Banquo aren't sure whether they are <u>real</u> or <u>made of air</u>. They speak in <u>shorter</u> lines that <u>rhyme</u> — unlike all the other characters — and that makes them sound different, and a bit <u>spooky</u>.

2) The Witches can <u>see the future</u>. And they conjure up <u>visions</u> that warn Macbeth. Everything they say <u>comes true</u> in the play, except the prediction about <u>Banquo's children</u> getting the throne — but that eventually came true in <u>real life</u> too.

3) Even though everything they say turns out to be <u>right</u>, the Witches are often seen as <u>evil</u>. That's because their prediction in Act 1 <u>tempts</u> Macbeth to murder Duncan. And in Act 4 they <u>lead</u> him into a <u>false sense of security</u> — by showing visions which they know he will <u>misinterpret</u>.

So can you tell me what'll win the 3.30 at Haydock?

4) <u>Hecate</u> is a goddess — she's kind of the <u>Witches' boss</u>. Don't worry too much about her.

Macduff — that'd be a sub-standard burger...

Macduff and Lady Macduff have an <u>important role</u> as <u>nice people</u> — in contrast to Macbeth and Lady Macbeth. And the <u>Weird Sisters</u> are the ones who <u>start</u> all the trouble in the first place.

The Less Important People

Now you know who everyone <u>important</u> is. The other characters in the play are <u>minor</u>.
But you'd better know <u>who they are</u>, just so you don't get <u>confused</u> if one appears in the SAT.

There's a Random Bunch of Noblemen

1) Lenox, Rosse, Menteith, Angus and Caithness are all <u>Thanes</u> — Scottish noblemen. None of them are <u>complicated</u> characters, and you don't really need to worry about <u>which is which</u>.

Which one am I again?

Aren't you Angus?

Hang on, then, so who am I?

2) They're basically there to <u>move the story along</u> and show how <u>power shifts</u> during the play. They're always around whenever anything happens, discussing it.

3) But there's a hint that Rosse <u>has his doubts</u> about Macbeth. He discusses how <u>terrible</u> the murder was with another minor character, a random <u>Old Man</u>. By the end of Act 3, Lenox <u>slags</u> Macbeth off to another <u>Lord</u>.

4) In Act 4 Rosse <u>warns</u> Lady Macduff to flee from Macbeth's troops. He pops up in England, giving Macduff the <u>bad news</u> and joining the <u>plot</u> against Macbeth. And by Act 5 the Thanes are all fighting in <u>Malcolm's army</u>, showing that Macbeth has <u>lost his grip</u> on power. Malcolm rewards them by making them <u>Earls</u>.

And Finally — The Other Minor Characters

1) The <u>Porter</u> appears in Act 2. He's <u>supposed to be funny</u>, rabbiting on about getting drunk. Back in Shakespeare's day, every play had to have a clown-like character to <u>amuse</u> the crowd, even if he <u>didn't really fit in</u> with the rest of the play — like the Porter.

2) Two <u>Murderers</u> appear in Act 3. They are <u>hired killers</u>. Macbeth persuades them to <u>kill Banquo</u> and his son, Fleance. Macbeth sends a <u>third murderer</u> along to make sure they do it properly — they kill Banquo but still <u>mess up</u> and let Fleance escape.

I tell you, mate, this job's murder.

3) <u>Siward</u> is an English Lord. He's a <u>great fighter</u> and he helps Malcolm defeat Macbeth in the war in Act 5. He's got a son, <u>Young Siward</u>, who is killed in battle by Macbeth. Siward shows how important <u>honour</u> and <u>bravery</u> are to him by saying he's glad that his son died a <u>good death</u>.

4) <u>Seyton</u> looks after Macbeth's armour for him in Act 5. And that's about it — apart from a couple of <u>Doctors</u>, some <u>Soldiers</u> and <u>Messengers</u>, and the <u>Gentlewoman</u> who's with Lady Macbeth when she goes mad. These are <u>really minor</u> characters — not very important at all.

Scottish Lords — a thane in the neck for Macbeth...

Now you know who everyone is. Don't forget, it's <u>more important</u> to know a lot about the <u>major</u> characters than the <u>minor</u> ones — but you do need to know how the minor ones <u>fit into the plot</u>.

Revision Summary

These questions will help you make sure you know exactly <u>who</u> all the characters are and <u>what</u> <u>they're like</u>. That's dead important, so don't skip it, whatever you do.

1) What's the main emotion that leads Macbeth to murder other people besides Duncan?
   a) ambition, b) fear, c) his love of cheesecake.

2) What happens to Macbeth when his conscience gets to him the most?

3) Who does Macbeth come to rely on instead of his wife?

4) What does Macbeth try to do when he hears predictions that he doesn't like?

5) Does it work?

6) What will Macbeth be in Lady Macbeth's eyes if he doesn't murder Duncan?

7) Why does Lady Macbeth want to be "unsexed"? (It's a bit sexist, this one.)

8) What does she try to do to get rid of her guilt when she's gone mad?

9) What is Duncan's biggest failing?

10) What's the difference between Macbeth's and Banquo's reactions to what the witches say about them?

11) Why does Malcolm become suspicious, even of Macduff?

12) What's Macduff's big mistake?

13) How does Malcolm test Macduff's allegiance?

14) Why are the witches deceitful, even though they actually tell Macbeth the truth?

15) Do the witches have any nice qualities?

16) What do Rosse and Lenox gradually realise?

17) Who's the only "funny" character in the play?

Section 3 — The Characters

The Supernatural

Some of the stuff in Macbeth seems pretty <u>weird</u> — like all those <u>witches</u> and <u>ghosts</u>.
That's because it was written <u>ages ago</u> — about <u>1600</u>.

People Believed in the Supernatural

If <u>you</u> had seen witches in the night, you might have been tempted to think they were just some
people in <u>fancy dress</u> trying to <u>scare</u> you, but in Shakespeare's day, they were totally <u>believable</u>.

Hi guys!   Aaargh!!! Witches!

The new broomcopters gave the
triplets a great idea for a joke.

Macbeth and Banquo are <u>confused</u> by the apparitions and
don't know whether they've been <u>dreaming</u> or <u>going mad</u> —
it's not exactly <u>usual</u> to see a <u>witch</u>. But they do think it's <u>possible</u>.

They Thought Powers to see the Future Came From the Devil

> Banquo: What! can the Devil speak true?
>
> Act 1, Scene 3, line 105

You are going to meet a tall, dark stranger...

It was a <u>common belief</u> that knowledge
of the future could only come from the <u>Devil</u>.
The witches in *Macbeth* are certainly <u>demonic</u> enough.

Notice that it's <u>not until</u> Macbeth meets the <u>Witches</u> that he finds himself <u>lured</u> by <u>evil</u>.
They say he will become <u>King</u>, and <u>immediately</u> he starts thinking of <u>murdering</u> Duncan.

The Witches' predictions of <u>greatness</u> are <u>true</u>, but what
they <u>don't</u> tell him is the <u>price</u> he will have to pay.

Just sign here, and the keys
to the royal palace are yours!

Banquo's Ghost — is it Real?

It seems pretty weird that <u>nobody</u> sees Banquo's ghost apart from <u>Macbeth</u>
— and that's in a room <u>full</u> of people. Does that mean he's just <u>imagining</u> it?

But I'm real!

No you're not. You're a
figment of my imagination.

Maybe, but if witches <u>exist</u>, why not <u>ghosts</u> — and
why shouldn't they be able to <u>choose</u> who sees them?

Remember that the
ghost <u>reappears</u>
later, <u>with</u> the sisters.

I never dye my hair — it's super-natural...

Macbeth isn't <u>just</u> about <u>magic</u> — but the witches and ghosts are pretty <u>important</u>.
They're part of <u>Macbeth's struggle</u> between <u>good</u> and <u>evil</u>. And they seemed <u>real</u> in 1600.

Kings in Scotland

Macbeth was written in about <u>1600</u>, but it's set even earlier — about <u>1050</u>. Here's a bit of <u>historical background</u>. Don't skip this or you might get confused...

Scotland <u>was an</u> Independent Country

Macbeth is set in the <u>time</u> when Scotland was a <u>separate country</u> from England.

> Scotland was ruled by <u>kings</u>.

All mine!

The King Chose <u>his</u> Successor

It looks <u>strange</u> to us that Macbeth <u>suddenly</u> becomes King, although he's <u>not</u> the <u>heir</u> to the throne.

But in Scotland, the successor <u>didn't</u> have to be the King's <u>eldest son</u>, even though in <u>practice</u> it often was.

> <u>Duncan</u> does choose his eldest son as his heir, but <u>Macbeth</u> is <u>next in line</u> after Malcolm and Donalbain. So he <u>frames</u> them — and gets the <u>throne</u>.

He was Duncan's cousin.

No, I'm afraid you're not the hare to the throne either.

People would Plot to Become King Themselves

Because succession wasn't set in <u>stone</u>, people could become King by <u>devious</u> means.

Macbeth gains the throne by <u>killing</u> the King and <u>laying the blame</u> on others. The way Macbeth becomes King and manages to escape <u>suspicion</u> is all a bit <u>weird</u> — but not that unusual in those days.

<u>Gradually</u>, other characters <u>realise</u> Macbeth is not a <u>true</u> king — his <u>evil</u> actions betray him.

So I killed a few people. That's just one of the things a king has to do.

Kings were supposed to be <u>morally superior</u> beings — like Duncan, and <u>Edward</u> the Confessor (King of England).

However, he's still <u>powerful</u> and commands <u>loyalty</u> — people had to <u>swear</u> loyalty to the King.

Macbeth loved Elvis — he wanted to be King...

Seems like a <u>hazardous</u> job being King — you'd need a good <u>bodyguard</u>. It <u>wasn't just</u> about <u>power</u>, though — people thought some men <u>deserved</u> to rule and others <u>didn't</u>. Macbeth didn't...

Who Has Power Apart From the King

Noblemen in Scotland had a chance of moving up the power structure.

A Thane is a Scottish Version of a Lord

Don't be put off by the word thane. That just means a kind of Lord.

Each thane has an area where he has power.

Not all thanes have the same amount of power.

Och aye!

A kind of Scottish Lord

For example, Macbeth is Thane of Glamis at the beginning, but then he becomes Thane of Cawdor as well — meaning that he's got power over two areas. Not bad going...

Thanes can Gain or Lose Power

No Ken, that's the palace cat again.

Die, traitor!

The way to become a thane — or to become a more powerful one — is to impress the King, usually by serving him well in battle.

Macbeth is really in Duncan's good books at the start of the play, and he gains power — another title — as a reward for fighting bravely. To climb even higher, he bumps off Duncan.

At times, Ken was a little too keen to serve the King.

Macbeth is next in line because the immediate heirs are suspected of murdering their father.

Rosse: Then 'tis most like
The sovereignty will fall upon Macbeth.
Act 2, Scene 4, lines 29-30

At the end of the play, the new King, Malcolm, is so pleased with his thanes that he makes them earls — an even greater honour.

Thane — an earl-y version of Lord...

That's all you really need to know — most of the characters are noble, and power can shift hands — like in the play, from Duncan to Macbeth, then from Macbeth to Malcolm. Not so hard really.

What Happens — Act 1, Scenes 1 & 2

You'll never <u>really</u> understand your set scenes unless you get to know the story of the <u>whole</u> <u>play</u>. Learn it here.

Scene 1 — The <u>Witches</u> Agree to Meet Macbeth

1 <u>The Witches set the spooky mood</u>
The Witches agree to meet Macbeth after the battle is over.

They seem to know where Macbeth will be — they can see the future.

Scene 2 — <u>King Duncan</u> is Told About the <u>Battle</u>

The battle is between:

King's Scottish Army	VS	Rebel Army
Led by King Duncan. Macbeth and Banquo are on Duncan's side. All the other Scottish lords in the play are too.		Led by Macdonwald. The Norwegian ("Norweyan") army are on his side. So is the Thane of Cawdor.

(In some versions, the Captain is called "Sergeant" instead.)

1 <u>A brave Captain gives the latest news</u>
The Captain says the battle was close. But then Macbeth bravely fought his way to Macdonwald then killed him.

Macdonwald was getting reinforcements.

2 <u>Macbeth & Banquo beat the Norweyan Lord</u>
The Captain says the Norweyan Lord started a new attack. Macbeth and Banquo fought even harder.

He got reinforcements too.

3 <u>Rosse says the Thane of Cawdor is a traitor</u>
Rosse says that Macbeth fought against the Thane of Cawdor, and Duncan's army won the battle.

The Thane of Cawdor helped the Norwegians — even though he was supposed to be on Duncan's side.

4 <u>Macbeth will be the new Thane of Cawdor</u>
Duncan says the old Thane of Cawdor must die. He tells Rosse to go and tell Macbeth of his 'promotion'.

Cawdor's a villain.

He wants to reward Macbeth for fighting well.

What Happens — Act 1, Scenes 3 & 4

Scene 3 — The Witches' Predictions;
Macbeth is Made Thane of Cawdor

This bit is so that we know they have real magic powers.

He already is Thane of Glamis, but he doesn't know he's been promoted to Thane of Cawdor yet. Of course, the audience does know.

Duncan thinks you're ace.

Macbeth is dead surprised.

Banquo also talks to Macbeth a bit about whether they should now believe what the Witches said.

1 **The Witches have a chat**
They talk about some evil things they've done and will do.

2 **Macbeth and Banquo turn up**
The Witches call Macbeth Thane of Glamis, Thane of Cawdor and King. The Witches say Banquo won't be King, but his sons will be.

3 **Rosse and Angus tell Macbeth he's ace**
They say how King Duncan is pleased with him, and that he's the new Thane of Cawdor.

4 **Macbeth talks to himself a bit**
He's thinking that because one thing the witches said came true, maybe he really is going to be King.

Hail! Hail! Hail!

They don't know whether to believe this stuff or not.

It already occurs to him he might have to murder to be King — which he calls a "horrible" idea. But he also wonders if it might happen by itself.

Scene 4 — King Duncan Welcomes Macbeth;
Malcolm is now Heir to the Throne

1 **The old Thane of Cawdor is dead**
Duncan says he used to trust him.

2 **Duncan praises Macbeth and Banquo**
They reply very respectfully and loyally.

3 **Duncan invites himself to Macbeth's place**
Eeeek!

4 **Malcolm is made Prince of Cumberland**
Macbeth knows this could get in the way of him (Macbeth) becoming King.

That's ironic, because Duncan shouldn't trust Macbeth either.

He's Thane of Cawdor and you're Prince of Cumberland.

That's like being Prince of Wales nowadays — he'll be the next King.

Witches are all alike — I can't tell which is which...

The scene's now set for a bit of action. Macbeth's been told he'll be King, but Duncan and Malcolm stand in his way. Banquo's kids look like a threat to him too. So murder might be the answer...

What Happens — Act 1, Scenes 5, 6 & 7

The next three scenes are all at Macbeth's Castle — Macbeth & Lady Macbeth make their plan...

Scene 5 — Lady Macbeth Decides Duncan Must Die

1 **Lady Macbeth reads Macbeth's letter**
He wrote about what the Witches told him, and that the Thane of Cawdor bit has already happened.

2 **She decides Macbeth will be King**
She thinks he should do whatever it takes to achieve it.

3 **A messenger says Duncan is coming**
Lady Macbeth thinks this is their chance to kill him.

4 **Macbeth comes in**
She tells him that he has to pretend to be nice, but be nasty underneath.

She reckons Macbeth might be a bit too weak though — that she'll have to persuade him.

She gives a little speech asking the "spirits" to make her evil, and asking the dark of the night to hide the murder she's planning.

Lady Macbeth says she'll work out what to do tonight. She doesn't say they'll kill Duncan, but you can tell that's what she means.

Scene 6 — Duncan & the Lords Arrive at Macbeth's

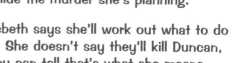

1 **Duncan and Banquo say it looks nice**
They think the castle's a nice place.

2 **Lady Macbeth welcomes Duncan...**
...all sweetly with respect and loyalty.

Wrong! No it isn't!

Two-faced cow!

Scene 7 — Macbeth and Lady M' Agree to Kill Duncan

He's worried because of:
1) the consequences (like being found out);
2) feeling guilty — Duncan is his friend, and a good king.

She makes it clear that she'd do anything to get what she wants — even kill a baby.

1 **Macbeth dithers — he's not sure**
He talks to himself in a long speech, about it being difficult to kill Duncan.

2 **Lady Macbeth persuades him again**
She tells him not to be a coward, and to carry out what he said he would.

3 **The plan to frame the "chamberlains"**
Lady Macbeth says she will get the servants drunk — then they can kill Duncan, and make it seem that the servants did it.

4 **Macbeth agrees to do it**
He thinks it's a good idea now.

The "chamberlains" are Duncan's servants (also known as grooms). Lady Macbeth is going to make sure they're asleep so they can't hear Duncan being killed. They'll use the servants' daggers, and cover the servants with blood. That way everyone will blame the servants, and not the Macbeths. Sneaky...

What Happens — Act 2, Scenes 1 & 2

Macbeth's in a <u>strange frame of mind</u> here. He even sees a <u>dagger</u> floating in mid-air — weird.
These are the scenes where Macbeth <u>kills Duncan</u> and Lady Macbeth covers the <u>servants</u> in blood.

Scene 1 — Banquo chats; Macbeth Sees the Dagger

He knows he's seeing things that aren't really there.

He makes a long fancy speech to himself about the planned murder.

1 <u>Banquo and Macbeth chat</u>
Banquo points out that one of the Witches' predictions has come true. Macbeth tells him they'll talk about it later.

2 <u>Macbeth sees a blood-covered dagger</u>
He says it's pointing the way to kill Duncan.

3 <u>He goes off to kill Duncan</u>
He gets a grip on himself, and sets off to do it.

Scene 2 — Macbeth Kills Duncan;
Lady Macbeth Frames His Servants

1 <u>Lady Macbeth talks to herself</u>
She says she's drugged the servants. She hears Macbeth say something off-stage and worries that something's gone wrong.

2 <u>Macbeth has killed Duncan</u>
He tells Lady Macbeth what happened.

3 <u>Donalbain and Malcolm woke up</u>
Macbeth saw them wake up and go back to sleep.

She's put the servants' daggers out ready, and says *she* would've killed Duncan then, but he looked like her Dad.

She's feeling dead nervous — not like she was in Act 1, Scenes 5 and 7.

Duncan's sons were in the next room.

I've done it!

Macbeth's feeling really bad. When Duncan's sons went back to sleep they said "Amen", but Macbeth couldn't say it. He heard a voice telling everyone he would "sleep no more".

He needs to wash his hands, and cover the servants with blood.

4 <u>Macbeth is being weird</u>
He feels all scared and anxious.

5 <u>Lady Macbeth tells him to get a grip</u>
She tells him not to worry, and to finish the plan — he's too scared though, so she goes.

zzzz
zzzz

Macbeth says some weird things about his bloody hands.
Lady Macbeth comes back and says with a quick wash they'll both be safe.

What Happens — Act 2, Scenes 3 & 4

Now for the <u>discovery</u> that Duncan's been <u>murdered</u>. Malcolm and Donalbain are <u>suspected</u>, and Macbeth gets away with his <u>dodgy</u> story about why he killed the <u>servants</u>.

Scene 3 — King Duncan is Found Dead

This bit's meant to be funny — the Porter makes loads of jokes.

This is tense, 'cos the audience knows Duncan's dead.

Oh no! Duncan's dead!

They can't trust the Scottish Lords.

1 <u>Macduff & Lenox knock at the gate</u>
The Porter talks to himself then lets them in.

2 <u>Macbeth greets Macduff and Lenox</u>
Macduff wants to see Duncan, and Macbeth plays it cool.

3 <u>Macduff's found King Duncan murdered</u>
He says how awful a sight it was, and calls for everyone to wake up.

4 <u>Macbeth and Lady Macbeth are 'sad'</u>
They pretend to be upset.

5 <u>Macbeth kills the servants</u>
Lenox says you could tell the servants were the murderers. Macbeth says he was so upset about Duncan that he killed the servants.

6 <u>Malcolm & Donalbain agree to scarper</u>
Donalbain reckons something nasty could happen to them too, so Malcolm will go to England, and Donalbain to Ireland.

You could argue that Macbeth means what he says — that he feels guilty already.

He gives an over-the-top speech about being really upset and hating the servants — he's trying hard to convince everyone.

Scene 4 — Macduff tells Rosse and Old Man the News

Stuff like horses eating each other — this adds to the spooky atmosphere.

Macduff says that the servants were the murderers. He also says Malcolm and Donalbain might be involved — they ran off like guilty men.

1 <u>Rosse and an Old Man chat</u>
About how dark it is, and unnatural things that animals have been doing.

2 <u>Macduff tells them the news...</u>
...about Duncan and the servants, and that Macbeth has been chosen as the new King.

3 <u>Macduff and Rosse go off</u>
Macduff is going home, and Rosse is going to see Macbeth being crowned.

Macbeth tried hard — he gave it a good stab...

This is a <u>spooky</u> part of the play — the Porter talks about <u>Hell</u>, and Lenox and the Old Man say the <u>weather</u> has been the <u>worst</u> they can ever remember. <u>Appropriate</u> for what's been going on...

What Happens — Act 3, Scenes 1, 2 & 3

*Scene 1 — Macbeth **Plots** Banquo's Murder*

1 **Banquo's suspicious**
Banquo's saying to himself how the Witches' prophecies have come true — but he reckons Macbeth played dirty to become King.

2 **Macbeth plans a big dinner**
Macbeth and Lady Macbeth tell Banquo he must be at their feast that night. Banquo says he's going out riding, but will be back.

Macbeth checks how far Banquo is going and whether he's taking his son, Fleance, with him. (Macbeth is planning to have them murdered while they're out riding.)

From what Macbeth says, you know he's talked to the murderers about this before, and has already convinced them they should hate Banquo.

3 **Macbeth waffles on**
He's worried that Banquo's son will become King.

4 **Macbeth plans Banquo's death**
He talks to two murderers, who agree to kill Banquo and Fleance.

Scene 2 — Macbeth and Lady Macbeth Chat

1 **Lady Macbeth tries to calm Macbeth**
Macbeth says he feels bad, and he's having bad dreams. Lady Macbeth says not to worry about it, and to make sure he looks calm and cheery at dinner.

She's worried he'll give himself away.

2 **They talk about Banquo**
Macbeth hints that he knows something awful's going to happen later that night. Lady Macbeth wants to know what, but Macbeth won't tell her.

Macbeth has already arranged Banquo's murder, but keeps it secret from Lady Macbeth. Earlier on he wasn't doing anything like that unless he was egged on by her.

*Scene 3 — Banquo **is** Murdered*

1 **The murderers meet up**
Macbeth has sent another one. The first two murderers wonder why Macbeth doesn't trust them.

Some people say that this is in the play so you know that Macbeth doesn't trust anyone any more.

2 **Banquo is murdered**
Banquo and Fleance ride in. Banquo is killed but Fleance gets away.

What Happens — Act 3, Scenes 4, 5 & 6

Scene 4 — Banquo's Ghost Turns up

1 Macbeth hears from the murderers
The feast is just starting. One of the murderers turns up and tells Macbeth Banquo's dead, but Fleance isn't.

2 Banquo's ghost appears
Macbeth tells the lords that he wishes Banquo was there. Banquo's ghost walks in and sits at Macbeth's seat. Macbeth sees him and goes barmy.

3 Lady Macbeth tries to cover up
Lady Macbeth tells the Thanes not to worry, as Macbeth is often like this, and he'll get better if they act normally.

Darn it!

No one else can see Banquo's ghost — only Macbeth.

At first Macbeth doesn't notice Banquo's ghost — he thinks there aren't any free seats. Then when Lenox points to his seat, he sees Banquo.

4 Banquo disappears... and appears again
The ghost disappears. Macbeth tells the Thanes that he gets ill like that sometimes. He drinks a toast to Banquo, whose ghost appears again.

5 Macbeth really flips out
Macbeth starts raving a bit — nearly giving away that he had Banquo killed. Lady Macbeth covers up for him, again saying he's often like this. The ghost disappears and Macbeth is better again.

6 Macbeth decides to see the Witches
Lady Macbeth tells the Thanes to leave, and they do. Macbeth asks why Macduff wasn't there, and says he's going to go to see the Witches.

Scene 5 — Hecate meets the Witches

1 Hecate is annoyed with the Witches
Hecate goes on about how the Witches have been meddling with Macbeth without her.

2 They plot more for the next day
Hecate tells the Witches to meet her in the morning, when Macbeth will come to them to ask about his destiny.

Hecate was the witches' leader — a kind of goddess of witchcraft.

It's pretty scary that Hecate already knows that Macbeth will come to see them.

Scene 6 — Lenox Talks to Another Lord

1 Lenox is suspicious
Lenox lets the other lord know that he suspects Macbeth.

2 Macduff has to gone see Malcolm
The lord tells Lenox that Macduff has gone to England to see Malcolm and convince him to raise an army to get rid of Macbeth.

This speech uses loads of irony. Lenox says that Fleance killed Banquo, and that Malcolm and Donalbain killed Duncan, but it's pretty obvious to the lord that Lenox doesn't really think that.

What Happens — Act 4, Scenes 1 & 2

Scene 1 — Macbeth sees the Witches

1 The Witches prepare a spell
The three Witches are putting some pretty grotty stuff into a cauldron. Hecate and three other witches turn up, they all sing a song, then Hecate and the three new witches go away.

Apparitions means ghosts.

2 Macbeth sees three apparitions
Macbeth turns up and says he's got some questions. He is shown three apparitions. They tell him to beware of Macduff, that no man born from a woman can harm him, and that he can't be beaten until Birnam Wood moves to Dunsinane Hill.

This bit is pretty freaky. Macbeth doesn't have to ask his questions — the apparitions somehow already know them. Scary.

3 Macbeth is confident
Macbeth isn't too worried about Macduff, because everyone's born from a woman, and woods can't move. He says he'll kill Macduff anyway, to be sure.

Even worse, some are carrying the orbs and sceptres that mean they're kings of England as well as Scotland.

4 Banquo's descendants shall be kings
Macbeth insists that the Witches let him know if Banquo's descendants will be kings. He sees a vision of eight of them, all wearing crowns. The last one is holding a mirror, which shows even more kings.

5 Lenox turns up
The Witches do a weird dance and disappear. Lenox arrives — he hasn't seen the Witches. He tells Macbeth that Macduff has gone to England. Macbeth says he'll have Macduff's family killed.

Scene 2 — Murderers go to Kill Macduff's Family

1 Rosse is defending Macduff to Lady Macduff
Lady Macduff slags off Macduff to Rosse for going to England. Rosse says Macduff is being wise, then goes. Macduff's son isn't worried, but Lady Macduff says her husband's a traitor.

2 Murderers turn up
A messenger arrives and tells Lady Macduff to run away. She has a bit of a strop and says it's not fair. Murderers arrive and kill Macduff's son. Lady Macduff sticks up for Macduff at the last minute, then she runs off (followed by a murderer).

What Happens — Act 4, Sc. 3 & Act 5, Sc. 1

Scene 3 — Malcolm is Going to Attack Macbeth

1 Macduff talks to Malcolm
Macduff tries to talk Malcolm into fighting Macbeth to become King of Scotland, but Malcolm pretends he thinks that he would be even worse than Macbeth. Macduff says that in that case Malcolm's not fit to live.

2 Malcolm reveals his plans
Malcolm tells Macduff that he was only testing him, to check he wasn't a spy from Macbeth. He's planning to attack Macbeth with help from the English.

3 A doctor praises the English King
A doctor walks in, says the English King has cured some people by touching them — then he leaves.

4 Rosse has bad news for Macduff
Rosse turns up from Scotland. Macduff asks how his wife and kids are. At first Rosse says they're fine, but then he tells him they've been killed. Malcolm and Macduff talk about revenge.

Act 5

Scene 1 — Lady Macbeth Loses her Marbles

1 A doctor and a servant watch Lady Macbeth
A servant refuses to repeat what she heard Lady Macbeth say while sleepwalking. Then Lady Macbeth appears — sleepwalking.

2 Lady Macbeth pretty much gives herself away
Lady Macbeth seems to be re-living the murders, and yaps on about blood. When Lady Macbeth has gone back to bed, the doctor tells the servant to keep an eye on her.

It could be dangerous for the servant to tell people she heard Lady Macbeth talking about the murders. Lady Macbeth might have her killed too.

She's nuts mate.

What Happens — Act 5, Scenes 2, 3, 4 & 5

Scene 2 — Some Thanes Join with Malcolm

1 Menteith, Caithness, Angus and Lenox meet
They talk about Malcolm and the army he's brought with him. They insult Macbeth, and go to help Malcolm.

They mention that Malcolm is near Birnam Wood (that's the wood the Witches said must move before Macbeth could be defeated). It's getting creepy...

Scene 3 — An Army's a-Coming...

1 A servant tells Macbeth an army's near
Macbeth is confident. A servant tells him that a force of 10 000 English are coming. Macbeth says he's not scared, because he can't be killed by any man born from a woman. He also says he's weary of life anyway.

2 Lady Macbeth is getting worse
A doctor says that Lady Macbeth is losing her mind. Macbeth is not too bothered. He puts his armour on, ready for a fight.

Scene 4 — Birnam Wood Marches

1 The English Army gets to Birnam Wood
Malcolm and his army are at Birnam Wood. Malcolm says every man should cut a branch and carry it, so you can't tell how many of them there are.

This is eerie. After hearing this, we know that Birnam Wood is going to move. Macbeth could be in trouble...

Scene 5 — Lady Macbeth Dies

1 Lady Macbeth dies
Macbeth says he can win a siege. He hears a cry and is told Lady Macbeth is dead. He's still not that bothered.

2 Birnam Wood is seen to be moving
A messenger arrives and says it looks like Birnam Wood is moving. Macbeth is worried. He now decides that they'll attack rather than trying to survive a siege.

Macbeth is planning to stay safe inside his castle, and let the English army surround it. He reckons they'll run out of food and become ill.

What Happens — Act 5, Scenes 6, 7, 8 & 9

Scene 6 — ATTACK!

1 Malcolm's army attacks
Malcolm tells everyone to put down their branches and fight. Siward and his son are to lead, followed by Malcolm and Macduff.

In some versions of the play scenes 6, 7, 8 and 9 are all run into one scene. In some other versions 6 is separate, but 7, 8 and 9 are one scene.

Scene 7 — Macbeth Kills Siward's Son

1 Macbeth kills Young Siward
Macbeth fights Young Siward and wins. Afterwards Macbeth says that the young man had no chance, because he was born of woman.

2 Macduff wants to kill Macbeth
Macduff talks to himself, saying that he doesn't want to fight anyone but Macbeth, and he doesn't want Macbeth to be killed by anyone else.

Gotcha!

Rats!

Scene 8 — Macbeth is Killed

1 Macduff finds Macbeth
Macduff finds Macbeth, but Macbeth says he doesn't want to fight, because he's already killed Macduff's family. Macduff attacks him anyway.

Maybe the real reason Macbeth doesn't want to fight is that he remembers the Witches telling him to beware of Macduff.

2 Macduff kills Macbeth
Macbeth says he can't be killed by anyone born from a woman. Macduff replies that he wasn't born, he was cut out from his mother. Macbeth gets scared, and says he doesn't want to fight. Macduff says if he doesn't he'll be kept prisoner. They fight and Macbeth is killed.

He was born by Caesarian.

Hurrah!

Scene 9 — The End

1 Siward finds out his son is dead
Malcolm and Siward find out from Rosse that young Siward is dead. Siward checks that his son wasn't running away, but doesn't seem too bothered that he's dead.

2 Malcolm is the new King
Macduff turns up with Macbeth's head. Malcolm makes all the Thanes into Earls to reward them for helping him. Then he invites everyone to his coronation.

Not all of the prophecies have come true yet — Banquo's descendants aren't kings.

Revision Summary

Now some quick questions to check you know the story. Keep doing them until you're sure about <u>what happens</u> — that's vital if you want loads of marks.

1) Did people in Shakespeare's day believe witches could exist?

2) When was *Macbeth* set, and when was it written?

3) What is a thane?

4) What ace thing has Macbeth done to earn him the title of Thane of Cawdor?

5) Why does Macbeth become King of Scotland instead of Malcolm?

6) Why doesn't Lady Macbeth kill Duncan herself when she has the chance?

7) What two things make Macbeth worried <u>before</u> he decides to kill Duncan?

8) What two weird things does Macbeth see <u>apart</u> from the witches?

9) Banquo suspects Macbeth of having bumped off Duncan. What other reason is there why he becomes the next murder victim?

10) What part does Lady Macbeth have in the murder of Banquo and the later murders?

11) Why has Macduff gone to England?

12) What two things do the Witches say to Macbeth that make him think he's unbeatable?

13) Why does Macbeth have Macduff's family murdered rather than Macduff himself?

14) How does Malcolm test whether Macduff is genuine, before they decide to raise an army and attack Macbeth?

15) What two things happen to Lady Macbeth in the end?

16) How is it possible that Birnam Wood comes to Dunsinane?

17) Who is "not born of woman" and why?

18) Why would Macduff have particular reason to want to kill Macbeth?

19) How does Malcolm reward the thanes for fighting for him against Macbeth?

I understand your story - that sort of thing happens to me all the time.

The set scenes are the only scenes you need to know in real detail.
Make sure you know Act 1 Scene 3 and Act 3 Scene 1 inside out.

> The first bit of the scene is just the Witches going on about some evil witchy stuff. It's not important for the plot, but I guess it shows you that the Witches are nasty. See P.20 for a quick summary.

ACT 1 SCENE 3
A heath

Thunder. Enter the three WITCHES.

FIRST WITCH   Where hast thou been, sister?

SECOND WITCH   Killing swine.

THIRD WITCH   Sister, where thou?

FIRST WITCH   A sailor's wife had chestnuts in her lap
And munched, and munched, and munched.
                              'Give me', quoth I.
'Aroint thee, witch!' the rump-fed ronyon cries.   5
Her husband's to Aleppo gone, master o'th'Tiger:
But in a sieve I'll thither sail,
And like a rat without a tail,
I'll do, I'll do, and I'll do.

SECOND WITCH   I'll give thee a wind.   10

FIRST WITCH   Thou'rt kind.

THIRD WITCH   And I another.

FIRST WITCH   I myself have all the other,
And the very ports they blow,
All the quarters that they know   15
I'th'shipman's card.
I'll drain him dry as hay:
Sleep shall neither night nor day
Hang upon his penthouse lid;
He shall live a man forbid.   20
Weary sennights nine times nine,
Shall he dwindle, peak, and pine.
Though his bark cannot be lost,
Yet it shall be tempest-tossed.
Look what I have.   25

SECOND WITCH   Show me, show me.

FIRST WITCH   Here I have a pilot's thumb,
Wrecked as homeward he did come.

Drum within

THIRD WITCH   A drum, a drum!
Macbeth doth come.   30

ALL   The weïrd sisters, hand in hand,
Posters of the sea and land,
Thus do go, about, about,
Thrice to thine, and thrice to mine,
And thrice again, to make up nine.   35
Peace — the charm's wound up.

Enter MACBETH and BANQUO.

MACBETH   So foul and fair a day I have not seen.

quoth I = I said

5 '"Get lost, witch!" shouted the spoilt cow.'

6 'Her husband's captain of the 'Tiger', and he's gone to Aleppo.'

7-8 People believed witches could turn into animals (including ones without tails), and sail in sieves.

10, 12 The other Witches will help make winds blow against the captain's ship.

14-16 'Winds will blow from all ports and from all corners of the compass.'

shipman's card = compass

18-24 'The storms will stop the captain sleeping for weeks and weeks, so he'll get all weak. His ship won't sink, but it'll be thrown about in storms.'

penthouse lid = eyelid

sennights = 7 nights (a week)

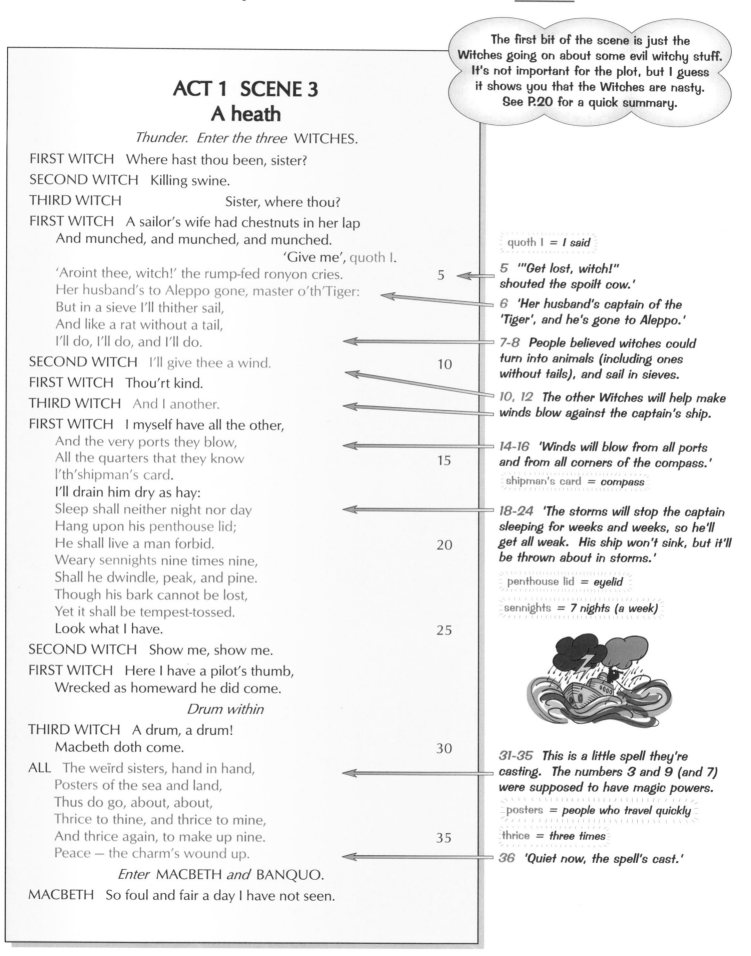

31-35 This is a little spell they're casting. The numbers 3 and 9 (and 7) were supposed to have magic powers.

posters = people who travel quickly

thrice = three times

36 'Quiet now, the spell's cast.'

38-42 *'What are these weird looking things, that don't look like Earth-dwellers, but are on the Earth? Are you alive, or are you something humans can talk to?'*

BANQUO   How far is't called to Forres? What are these,
So withered and so wild in their attire,
That look not like th'inhabitants o'th'earth,   40
And yet are on't? Live you, or are you aught
That man may question? You seem to understand me,
By each at once her choppy finger laying
Upon her skinny lips; you should be women,

44-46 *'You must be women, but as you've got beards, that's hard to believe.'*

And yet your beards forbid me to interpret   45
That you are so.

MACBETH   Speak if you can: what are you?

47-49 *This bit's dead important — the Witches call Macbeth Thane of Glamis (which he knows he is), then Thane of Cawdor (which he is but he doesn't know it yet), and then say he'll be King.*

FIRST WITCH   All hail Macbeth! Hail to thee, Thane of Glamis.
SECOND WITCH   All hail Macbeth! Hail to thee, Thane of Cawdor.
THIRD WITCH   All hail Macbeth that shalt be King hereafter!

Glamis is pronounced strangely: it's Glarms, not Gla-miss.

BANQUO   Good sir, why do you start, and seem to fear   50
Things that do sound so fair? I'th'name of truth

52-53 *'Are you imaginary or real?'*

Are ye fantastical, or that indeed
Which outwardly ye show? My noble partner

54-55 *'saying Macbeth is Thane of Cawdor and will be King'*

You greet with present grace and great prediction
Of noble having and of royal hope   55
That he seems rapt withal. To me you speak not.

rapt withal = completely spellbound

If you can look into the seeds of time
And say which grain will grow and which will not,

59-60 *Banquo wants to know about his own future.*

Speak then to me, who neither beg nor fear
Your favours nor your hate.   60

FIRST WITCH   Hail!
SECOND WITCH   Hail!
THIRD WITCH   Hail!

64-66 *Banquo is less than Macbeth because he won't be King. But he's also more, because his sons will be kings, and he's a better man too.*

FIRST WITCH   Lesser than Macbeth, and greater.
SECOND WITCH   Not so happy, yet much happier.   65
THIRD WITCH   Thou shalt get kings, though thou be none.
So all hail Macbeth and Banquo!

FIRST WITCH   Banquo and Macbeth, all hail!

MACBETH   Stay, you imperfect speakers. Tell me more.

70-74 *Macbeth inherited the title Thane of Glamis from his dad, Sinel. He doesn't see how he can be Thane of Cawdor, though, and thinks being King is unlikely.*

By Sinel's death, I know I am Thane of Glamis,   70
But how of Cawdor? The Thane of Cawdor lives
A prosperous gentleman, and to be king
Stands not within the prospect of belief,
No more than to be Cawdor. Say from whence

74-75 *'Tell me where you got this info from'*

You owe this strange intelligence, or why   75
Upon this blasted heath you stop our way
With such prophetic greeting? Speak, I charge you.
                    WITCHES *vanish.*

BANQUO   The earth hath bubbles, as the water has,
And these are of them. Whither are they vanished?

whither = to where

corporal = of flesh and blood

MACBETH   Into the air, and what seemed corporal,   80
Melted, as breath into the wind. Would they had stayed.

would = I wish

BANQUO   Were such things here as we do speak about?

82-84 *'Were they really here, or have we lost our marbles?'*

Or have we eaten on the insane root,
That takes the reason prisoner?

MACBETH   Your children shall be kings.

BANQUO   You shall be King.   85

MACBETH   And Thane of Cawdor too: went it not so?

BANQUO   To th'self same tune and words — who's here?

Enter ROSSE and ANGUS

ROSSE   The King hath happily received, Macbeth,
    The news of thy success, and when he reads
    Thy personal venture in the rebels' sight,   90
    His wonders and his praises do contend
    Which should be thine or his. Silenced with that,
    In viewing o'er the rest o'th'selfsame day,
    He finds thee in the stout Norwegian ranks,
    Nothing afeard of what thyself didst make,   95
    Strange images of death. As thick as tale
    Came post with post, and every one did bear
    Thy praises in his kingdom's great defence,
    And poured them down before him.

ANGUS   We are sent
    To give thee from our royal master thanks;   100
    Only to herald thee into his sight,
    Not pay thee.

ROSSE   And for an earnest of a greater honour,
    He bade me, from him, call thee Thane of Cawdor:
    In which addition, hail most worthy Thane,   105
    For it is thine.

BANQUO   What, can the devil speak true?

MACBETH   The Thane of Cawdor lives. Why do you dress me
    In borrowed robes?

ANGUS   Who was the Thane, lives yet,
    But under heavy judgement bears that life
    Which he deserves to lose.   110
    Whether he was combined with those of Norway,
    Or did line the rebel with hidden help
    And vantage, or that with both he laboured
    In his country's wrack, I know not,
    But treasons capital, confessed and proved,   115
    Have overthrown him.

MACBETH *(Aside)*   Glamis, and Thane of Cawdor:
    The greatest is behind. —Thanks for your pains. —
    (To Banquo) Do you not hope your children shall be kings,
    When those that gave the Thane of Cawdor to me
    Promised no less to them?

BANQUO   That, trusted home,   120
    Might yet enkindle you unto the crown,
    Besides the Thane of Cawdor. But 'tis strange,
    And oftentimes, to win us to our harm,
    The instruments of darkness tell us truths,
    Win us with honest trifles — to betray's   125
    In deepest consequence.
    Cousins, a word, I pray you.

MACBETH *(Aside)*   Two truths are told,
    As happy prologues to the swelling act
    Of the imperial theme. — I thank you, gentlemen. —

Rosse and Angus come to tell Macbeth that he's the new Thane of Cawdor. Macbeth starts wondering if what the Witches said will come true after all.

88-92 'The King's heard about how bravely you fought in the battle. When he hears the detail he'll be even more impressed, and hardly know what to give you as a reward.'

post with post = message after message

101 'to be your official escort to the King'

106 Banquo realises the Witches' first prediction has come true.

107-108 'How can I be Thane of Cawdor when the old one's still alive?'

108-116 'The old Thane of Cawdor is going to be killed soon. I don't know the details of what he did, but he's confessed and it's been proved he was a traitor.'

wrack = ruin

117 'The greatest is yet to come.'

120-126 'If you believe what they said, you're going to be King as well as Thane of Cawdor. On the other hand, evil creatures sometimes get people to trust them by saying a few things that are true — then get them into big trouble.'

127-129 'The two true things the Witches said are just the build-up to the important bit about being King.'

This supernatural soliciting 130
Cannot be ill, cannot be good. If ill,
Why hath it given me earnest of success,
Commencing in a truth? I am Thane of Cawdor.
130-141 'The predictions can't be good,
and they can't be bad. If they're bad, why If good, why do I yield to that suggestion,
has part of it come true? But if they're Whose horrid image doth unfix my hair 135
good, why do I keep thinking of killing And make my seated heart knock at my ribs
Duncan, which really scares me? Nothing Against the use of nature? Present fears
is as frightening as my own imagination. Are less than horrible imaginings.
My thoughts are taking me over and My thought, whose murder yet is but fantastical,
stopping me doing anything' Shakes so my single state of man that function 140
Is smothered in surmise, and nothing is,
But what is not.

rapt = deep in thought

BANQUO   Look how our partner's rapt.

143-144 'If my fate is to be King, fate MACBETH   If chance will have me King, why, chance may crown me,
may make me King, even if I do nothing.' Without my stir.

144-146 'Macbeth's stunned BANQUO   New honours come upon him
by the good news.' Like our strange garments, cleave not to their mould, 145
But with the aid of use.

146-147 'Whatever MACBETH   Come what come may,
happens will happen.' Time and the hour runs through the roughest day.

BANQUO   Worthy Macbeth, we stay upon your leisure.

MACBETH   Give me your favour. My dull brain was wrought
149-152 'Sorry, I was miles away. With things forgotten. Kind gentlemen, your pains 150
I'll remember what you've done for Are registered where every day I turn
me. Let's go and see the King.' The leaf to read them. Let us toward the King.
(*To Banquo*) Think upon what hath chanced and, at more time,
153-155 'Think about The interim having weighed it, let us speak
what's happened and we'll Our free hearts each to other.
talk about it later.'

BANQUO   Very gladly. 155

MACBETH   Till then, enough. Come, friends.
                    Exeunt

ACT 3 SCENE 1
The royal palace at Forres

Enter BANQUO

BANQUO   Thou hast it now — King, Cawdor, Glamis, all,
As the weird women promised, and, I fear,
Thou play'dst most foully for't. Yet it was said
It should not stand in thy posterity,
But that myself should be the root and father   5
Of many kings. If there come truth from them —
As upon thee, Macbeth, their speeches shine —
Why, by the verities on thee made good,
May they not be my oracles as well,
And set me up in hope? But hush! No more.   10

Sennet sounded. Enter MACBETH, *as king,* LADY MACBETH,
as queen, LENOX, ROSS, *Lords, Ladies, and Attendants.*

MACBETH   Here's our chief guest.

LADY MACBETH   If he had been forgotten,
It had been as a gap in our great feast,
And all-thing unbecoming.

MACBETH   To-night we hold a solemn supper sir,
And I'll request your presence.

BANQUO   Let your highness   15
Command upon me, to the which my duties
Are with a most indissoluble tie
For ever knit.

MACBETH   Ride you this afternoon?

BANQUO   Ay, my good lord.

MACBETH   We should have else desired your good advice,   20
Which still hath been both grave and prosperous,
In this day's council, but we'll take to-morrow.
Is't far you ride?

BANQUO   As far, my lord, as will fill up the time
'Twixt this and supper. Go not my horse the better,   25
I must become a borrower of the night
For a dark hour or twain.

MACBETH   Fail not our feast.

BANQUO   My lord, I will not.

MACBETH   We hear, our bloody cousins are bestowed
In England and in Ireland, not confessing   30
Their cruel parricide, filling their hearers
With strange invention — but of that to-morrow,
When therewithal we shall have cause of state
Craving us jointly. Hie you to horse. Adieu,
Till you return at night. *Goes Fleance with you?*   35

BANQUO   Ay, my good lord, our time does call upon 's.

MACBETH   I wish your horses swift and sure of foot,
And so I do commend you to their backs. Farewell.

Exit BANQUO

Let every man be master of his time

1-3 'You've got it all now, Macbeth — king, Thane of Cawdor <u>and</u> Glamis — just as the witches promised, but I'm worried you've done something terrible to get it.'

stand in thy posterity = stay in your family

3-10 Banquo feels better, remembering that the Witches said he'd be the father of many kings. If what they said came true for Macbeth, then surely it will for him too.

sennet = trumpet fanfare

Banquo has been talking to himself. Now Macbeth and some others enter.

11-15 Macbeth and Lady Macbeth suck up to Banquo.

indissoluble = unbreakable

19,23,35 Macbeth is sneakily finding out what Banquo will be doing later on.

24-25 'I'll ride as far as I can between now and supper.'

27 'Don't miss our feast.'

our bloody cousins = Malcolm and Donalbain

29-32 'Malcolm and Donalbain have gone to England and Ireland, without confessing to their Dad's murder, and telling all kinds of awful lies — but we'll talk about that tomorrow.'

39-40 'Everyone occupy yourselves until 7pm.'

44 *'Are those men here to see me?'* ———→

without = **outside**

46 *'Just being King in name isn't enough —* ———→
I need to feel secure in my position.'

47-53 *Macbeth is worried about Banquo* ———→
— he is a brave and wise man and the only
man that Macbeth is afraid of.

Genius = **guardian angel**

54-55 *In Ancient Rome, Mark Antony*
and Octavius Caesar both wanted to be ———→
ruler, and Caesar won in the end.

55-58 *'Banquo didn't like it when the* ———→
Witches said I'd be King and he asked
them to speak to him too. Then they
said he'd be father of many kings.'

59-68 *'Having the crown is pointless*
if my sons don't succeed me. If it's
true, then I've done this dreadful thing ———→
and murdered Duncan for the sake of
Banquo's kids. I've turned peace to
hostility and have given my soul to the
devil — all for them!'

issue = **children**

eternal jewel = **soul**

69-70 *Macbeth thinks this is so* ———→
bad that he wants to challenge
fate to a fight to the death.

list = **jousting arena**

74-82 *When Macbeth spoke to the*
murderers the day before, he told ———→
them that Banquo is their enemy.

passed in probation = **looked over the proof**

Till seven at night. To make society   40
The sweeter welcome,
We will keep ourself till supper-time alone —
While then, God be with you!

      Exeunt all but MACBETH, *and a* SERVANT
          Sirrah, a word with you.
Attend those men our pleasure?

SERVANT   They are, my lord,
Without the palace gate.

MACBETH   Bring them before us.   45

        Exit SERVANT
To be thus is nothing but to be safely thus.
Our fears in Banquo
Stick deep, and in his royalty of nature
Reigns that which would be feared. 'Tis much he dares,
And, to that dauntless temper of his mind,   50
He hath a wisdom that doth guide his valour
To act in safety. There is none but he
Whose being I do fear, and, under him,
My Genius is rebuked; as, it is said,
Mark Antony's was by Caesar. He chid the sisters   55
When first they put the name of king upon me,
And bade them speak to him. Then prophet-like
They hailed him father to a line of kings —
Upon my head they placed a fruitless crown,
And put a barren sceptre in my gripe,   60
Thence to be wrenched with an unlineal hand,
No son of mine succeeding. If 't be so,
For Banquo's issue have I filed my mind,
For them the gracious Duncan have I murdered;
Put rancours in the vessel of my peace   65
Only for them, and mine eternal jewel
Given to the common enemy of man,
To make them kings, the seed of Banquo kings!
Rather than so, come fate into the list.
And champion me to the utterance! Who's there?   70

      Re-enter SERVANT, *with two* MURDERERS
Now go to the door, and stay there till we call.

        Exit SERVANT
Was it not yesterday we spoke together?

FIRST MURDERER   It was, so please your highness.

MACBETH   Well then, now
Have you considered of my speeches? Know
That it was he in the times past which held you   75
So under fortune, which you thought had been
Our innocent self — this I made good to you
In our last conference, passed in probation with you,
How you were borne in hand, how crossed, the instruments,
Who wrought with them, and all things else that might   80
To half a soul and to a notion crazed
Say 'Thus did Banquo.'

FIRST MURDERER   You made it known to us.

MACBETH   I did so, and went further, which is now
    Our point of second meeting. Do you find
    Your patience so predominant in your nature
    That you can let this go? Are you so gospelled   85
    To pray for this good man and for his issue,
    Whose heavy hand hath bowed you to the grave
    And beggared yours for ever?

FIRST MURDERER   We are men, my liege.

MACBETH   Ay, in the catalogue ye go for men,   90
    As hounds and greyhounds, mongrels, spaniels, curs,
    Shoughs, water-rugs and demi-wolves, are clept
    All by the name of dogs. The valued file
    Distinguishes the swift, the slow, the subtle,
    The housekeeper, the hunter, every one   95
    According to the gift which bounteous nature
    Hath in him closed, whereby he does receive
    Particular addition, from the bill
    That writes them all alike — and so of men.
    Now, if you have a station in the file,   100
    Not i' the worst rank of manhood, say 't,
    And I will put that business in your bosoms,
    Whose execution takes your enemy off,
    Grapples you to the heart and love of us,
    Who wear our health but sickly in his life,   105
    Which in his death were perfect.

SECOND MURDERER   I am one, my liege,
    Whom the vile blows and buffets of the world
    Have so incensed that I am reckless what
    I do to spite the world.

FIRST MURDERER   And I another
    So weary with disasters, tugged with fortune,
    That I would set my lie on any chance,   110
    To mend it, or be rid on't.

MACBETH   Both of you
    Know Banquo was your enemy.

BOTH MURDERERS.   True, my lord.

MACBETH   So is he mine; and in such bloody distance,
    That every minute of his being thrusts   115
    Against my near'st of life — and though I could
    With barefaced power sweep him from my sight
    And bid my will avouch it, yet I must not,
    For certain friends that are both his and mine,
    Whose loves I may not drop, but wail his fall   120
    Who I myself struck down; and thence it is,
    That I to your assistance do make love,
    Masking the business from the common eye
    For sundry weighty reasons.

SECOND MURDERER   We shall, my lord,
    Perform what you command us.

FIRST MURDERER   Though our lives —   125

83-89 Macbeth taunts the murderers, saying they're not man enough to take revenge on Banquo. 'Are you such wimps that you're going to let him get away with this?'

gospelled = religious

89 'Oi, we're not wimps, we're men!'

90-106 'You say you're men but, like dogs, there are lots of different types of man, each with different qualities. If you are high quality men then say it, and I'll help you to kill your enemy.'

clept = called

Come here, and I'll give you a kiss.

104 'You'll have my affection and gratitude'

106-109 'I've had such a horrible life that I'll do anything to get back at the world.'

109-112 'Same here.'

114-124 'Banquo is my enemy too — and such a bad one that he threatens my existence. I could just use my power to get rid of him openly but I won't, because we have mutual friends who I don't want to upset. So I'm getting you to help me, to keep his murder out of the public eye.'

Section 5 — The Set Scenes

126-130 *Macbeth interrupts the first Murderer, to give them the details about when and where to do the dirty deed.*

perfect spy o' the time = the exact time

something from = away from

132 *'Don't leave any clues or make any mistakes'*

133-136 *'His son, Fleance, is with him and I don't like him either, so kill him too.'*

MACBETH   Your spirits shine through you. Within this hour at most
I will advise you where to plant yourselves.
Acquaint you with the perfect spy o' the time,
The moment on't, for't must be done to-night,
And something from the palace, always thought   130
That I require a clearness — and with him
To leave no rubs nor botches in the work —
Fleance his son, that keeps him company,
Whose absence is no less material to me
Than is his father's, must embrace the fate   135
Of that dark hour. Resolve yourselves apart —
I'll come to you anon.
BOTH MURDERERS   We are resolved, my lord.
MACBETH   I'll call upon you straight. Abide within.
                    Exeunt MURDERERS
It is concluded. Banquo, thy soul's flight,
If it find heaven, must find it out to-night.   140
                    Exit

Planning and Structure

If you <u>plan</u> your essay first, you'll have <u>more</u> chance of getting <u>loads</u> of <u>marks</u>.

Before you Write, Make a Plan

I wish I was organised...

Planning means <u>organising</u> your material to help you write a clear answer that makes sense. A good plan turns that <u>heap of ideas</u> in your head into an <u>argument</u> supported by <u>points</u>.

Planning might seem a <u>pain</u> to do, but if you do it, you'll be <u>less</u> likely to get <u>lost</u> halfway through the essay.

You Need a Beginning, a Middle and an End

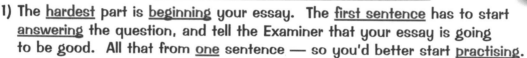

A good essay has a <u>beginning</u>, a <u>middle</u> and an <u>end</u>. Just like a good story.

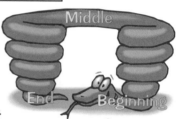

Just like me then.

1) The <u>hardest</u> part is <u>beginning</u> your essay. The <u>first sentence</u> has to start <u>answering</u> the question, and tell the Examiner that your essay is going to be good. All that from <u>one</u> sentence — so you'd better start <u>practising</u>.

2) The middle part of your essay <u>develops</u> your <u>argument</u> — this is where you make all your points. Follow your plan.

3) The end <u>sums up</u> the points you've made and <u>rounds</u> the essay <u>off</u> nicely.

Five Steps to Planning a Good Essay

① Work out <u>exactly</u> what the question is asking you to do. Find the <u>key words</u> and circle them.

② Read the <u>bits of the play</u> — highlight <u>quotations</u> you could use.

③ Jot down your <u>ideas</u> — from the bits of the play they <u>give</u> you, and from your <u>knowledge</u> of the <u>rest</u> of the play — and then put them into an <u>order</u>.

④ Decide what your <u>opinion</u> is, and how you can <u>use</u> your points to <u>support</u> it — to form an <u>argument</u>. Put your <u>best</u> point <u>first</u>.

⑤ Don't stick to your plan <u>blindly</u>. Your <u>best</u> ideas might come once you've <u>started</u> to write.

REMEMBER: if you're not sure what your opinion is, state the arguments for and against. Answer the question by comparing the views on each side.

Planning and Structure

Here are a few more handy tips which will help you in the exam...

Making Your Plan

This is the kind of thing you could write for a plan.
Don't bother writing in proper English — just get your ideas down.

You get 45 minutes for this question — spend at least 10 minutes reading and planning.

This essay's about how Macbeth decided to murder Duncan. So write down everything you think is relevant from the scenes.

Scribble down where you can get good quotes to back it all up.

Decide on the best order to write about your points in.

Write down any comments you've got about each one.

How does Macbeth persuade himself to murder Duncan and how does Lady Macbeth help to persuade him?

1. Macbeth's original thoughts
Act 1, Scene 7 — worried about consequences. Feels guilty — Duncan's a friend and a good king.

3. 2. Macbeth's final thoughts
Act 2, Scene 1 — sees the dagger, frightened, then convinces himself to murder Duncan.

2. 3. Lady Macbeth's persuasion
Act 1, Scene 7 — tells Macbeth not to be a coward, he can't love her if he won't do it, she'd do anything to get what she wants, suggests a plan.

Think about Style and Vocabulary

Use interesting words — the Examiner will get very bored if you overuse words like "nice" or phrases like "I think".

You must keep your style formal — this makes your argument more convincing and gets you even more marks.

If you think a passage is "poetic", "realistic" etc., remember to explain exactly why — with examples. Don't assume it's obvious to the Examiner.

Boring!
It was a nice day, and everyone had a nice time.

Keep bearing in mind the words used in the question. Using them in your essay will show you're keeping to the task and not getting lost.

What I think is, Macbeth had it coming to him, all them murders and stuff...

In my opinion, Macbeth's atrocious crimes make his end inevitable and just.

Wrong style   Right style

My essay blossomed — I plant it well...

Don't just launch straight in — take the time to plan. Once you've jotted some ideas down, you'll realise you have more to say than you thought — so there's less reason to panic. And let's face it, a structured essay will get more marks than one that goes all over the place...

Writing Your Answer

Once you've got a plan, you're <u>ready</u> to start writing.
Make your points as <u>clearly</u> as you can so the examiner knows what you're on about.

Write a *Simple* Opening Paragraph

Use the words of the task.

Do you think I'm too cute to be in this book? I do.

Start by using the exact <u>words of the task</u> in your introduction.

Your introduction <u>doesn't</u> have to be <u>long</u> at all. It's just there to show what your <u>basic answer</u> to the task is.

Start by leaving a little <u>gap</u> — and do the same for <u>each paragraph</u>.

> *How does Macbeth persuade himself to murder Duncan and how does Lady Macbeth help to persuade him?*
>   *In these scenes, Macbeth persuades himself to kill Duncan. Lady Macbeth helps and encourages him. She uses a combination of flattery and insults to persuade Macbeth, who has to convince himself that power is more important than a clear conscience.*
>   *At first, Macbeth was not convinced about...*

The first sentences use the <u>exact</u> words of the task.

The third sentence is a <u>straight answer</u> to the task.

When you've written your opening paragraph, just follow the order of the <u>plan</u>.

Use *Lots* of Tasty *Quotations*

You are <u>guaranteed</u> to get better marks if your answer's got some good quotes. Trouble is, you've got to <u>quote properly</u>. Here's how...

Copy down the <u>exact</u> words.

Start a new paragraph.

> *...and so he begins to change his mind.*
>   *Macbeth compliments Lady Macbeth on her courage and ambition:*
> *   Bring forth men-children only,*
> *For thy undaunted mettle should compose*
> *Nothing but males.*
>   *Act 1, Scene 7, 73-74*

Quotes <u>show</u> where your answer <u>comes from</u>.

Say <u>where</u> the quote comes from. Give the <u>line numbers</u> — and give the <u>scene</u> number, too.

Don't quote <u>more</u> than <u>two or three</u> lines at a time.

If the quote's less than a line you <u>won't</u> need to put it in a separate paragraph, but you <u>will</u> need to put it in quotation marks.

> *...Lady Macbeth asks if Macbeth is such a coward that he won't do what is needed to get what he wants*
> *"like the poor cat i'th'adage"...*

"Salt and Vinegar" — there's a tasty quote...

The examiners really are <u>dead keen</u> on quoting. If you don't quote at all, you'll get a <u>low mark</u>, no matter <u>how good</u> the <u>rest</u> of your answer is. Don't quote <u>huge chunks</u>, though — you only need a <u>couple of lines</u> to show where your answer comes from. It's all about striking a balance.

Concluding and Checking for Errors

Once you've made <u>all</u> your points, you need to <u>sum up</u> your answer and <u>check</u> it through.

Summing Up — Bringing Together the Key Points

① Start a new <u>paragraph</u> by going back to the <u>original question</u>.

② Restate the <u>main points</u> of your essay <u>briefly</u>.
This makes it clear how you've <u>answered</u> the question.

③ Don't go on and on, though. You must be <u>focused</u>.
Once you've <u>summed up</u>, write a final <u>sentence</u> to <u>conclude</u>.

The conclusion to my speech will be very concise - barely half an hour...

Go Over Your Essay When You've Finished

① Try to <u>leave time</u> at the end to <u>read through</u> your essay quickly.
Check that it <u>makes sense</u>, that you haven't got any facts wrong, and that it says what you <u>want</u> it to say.

Don't <u>scribble</u> or put <u>whitener</u> on mistakes — that's <u>messy</u> and you'll <u>lose marks</u>.

② Check the <u>grammar</u>, <u>spelling</u> and <u>punctuation</u>. If you find a <u>mistake</u>, put <u>brackets</u> round it, cross it out <u>neatly</u> with two lines through it and write the <u>correction</u> above.

Macbeth (Mcbath)

How many more times do I have to go over it?

③ If you've written something which isn't <u>clear</u>, put an <u>asterisk</u> * at the end of the sentence. Put another asterisk in the <u>margin</u> beside the sentence, and write what you <u>mean</u> in the margin.

He had him killed. | Macbeth wasn't nice to Banquo.

Don't Panic if You Realise You've Gone Wrong

If you realise you've <u>forgotten</u> something really <u>obvious</u> and <u>easy</u>, then write a <u>note</u> about it at the bottom of the <u>final</u> page, to tell the Examiner. If there's time, write an extra <u>paragraph</u>. You'll pick up marks for <u>noticing</u> your mistake.

<u>Never cross out</u> your <u>whole essay</u> if you realise it's wrong — that's just a <u>waste</u> of time. <u>Don't panic</u>, just <u>continue</u> the essay, <u>explaining</u> to the Examiner <u>why</u> it's wrong. If there's time, tell them what the <u>real answer</u> is.

Betsy still had loads of time...

<u>Don't give up</u> if you're running out of <u>time</u>: even if you only have <u>five minutes</u> left, that's still time to pick up <u>extra marks</u>.

Check, check, check — I must be rich...

You've almost <u>finished</u>. Keep your conclusions <u>to the point</u>, and <u>check</u> your essay so you don't <u>throw away</u> marks on <u>silly mistakes</u>. Keep a <u>clear head</u> right up to the end — then it's <u>teatime</u>.

Three Steps for an Essay

Now it's time for a detailed look at four kinds of question you might get. I'll start you off with the one that's probably easiest — when the question asks you to write about a character.

Here's an Example Question

Act 1 Scene 3, line 126 to the end of the scene
Act 1 Scene 7

In these extracts, Macbeth ponders over whether to kill Duncan.

How do Macbeth's thoughts and intentions change in these extracts?

Support your ideas by referring to the extracts.

Check Exactly What the Task is Asking For

It's a good idea to start by reading through the extracts.
Now have a good look at exactly what the question is asking you to do.

How do Macbeth's thoughts and intentions change in these extracts?

These are the most important words in the question.
This is what you have to write about.

1) Go through the extracts, underlining words that look like they'll help answer the question.

2) For this one, underline examples of Macbeth changing his mind and making new decisions.

3) Then go through again looking for any less obvious examples.

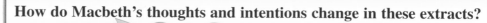

MACBETH   I am settled and bend up
Each corporal agent to this terrible feat.
Away, and mock the time with fairest show,
False face must hide what the false heart doth know.

Three Key Steps for Success

Here's what you do — take a step-by-step approach. These are the three steps.

① Read the question thoroughly. Make sure you know what it's really asking.

② Search through the scenes for examples of bits that are relevant to the question. Make notes on all the relevant bits.

③ Use the notes to write your answer.

In fact, these three steps are a darn good start when you're approaching any kind of question in your Shakespeare SAT — not just the ones that ask you to write about a character.

Three small steps — they're one giant leap...

Lucky old you — a whole section about the types of questions you get. Get that 3 step plan in your head and you're off to a great start. Read the question really thoroughly. Make notes on things you find that are relevant to the question. And use the notes to write your answer.

Writing About A Character

Characters — The Bigger Picture

Here are some <u>handy hints</u> to bear in mind when you're writing about a character.
Make sure you <u>look out</u> for these — you'll get <u>extra marks</u> if you spot this kind of stuff.

Some Characters Have More Than One Side

The major characters have <u>different sides</u> to their personality — they'd be pretty dull and <u>boring</u> if they didn't. If you forget that, their behaviour can seem <u>confusing</u>.

Take Macbeth — you need to remember he's full of <u>contradictions</u>. His <u>craving for power</u> makes him act <u>ruthlessly</u> but he's got enough of a conscience to make him feel <u>so bad</u> it almost drives him <u>insane</u>. He's <u>brave</u>, but he's <u>terrified</u> of losing his power.

If you didn't know this stuff, you'd never understand, say, why Macbeth reacts as he does in Act 3 Scene 4 — he's <u>pleased</u> when he hears Banquo's dead, <u>afraid</u> when he hears Fleance isn't, and <u>falls apart</u> when he sees Banquo's ghost.

Mervin definitely had <u>two sides</u>.

It's What They Do As Well As What They Say

It's easy just to look at the <u>words</u> the characters say, and forget that when it's <u>acted out</u> on stage they're <u>doing</u> stuff as well.

Suppose you're asked about Macbeth's behaviour in Act 2 Scene 2. Don't forget that when Macbeth first comes in, not only has he just <u>killed Duncan</u>, he's still <u>carrying the daggers</u> and he's got <u>blood</u> all over his hands. That shows you that he's in a <u>bit of a state</u>.

Know What Happens in the Rest of the Play

Although you'll only be asked about <u>one or two scenes</u>, it'll often help if you remember what happens in <u>other parts</u> of the play. That way you can put things in <u>context</u>.

Take Act 4 Scene 1 — it'll help you to write about Macbeth's reaction to the <u>apparitions</u> if you know the <u>reason</u> he believes them is that the Witches' predictions to him in <u>Act 1</u> came true. And <u>only</u> if you know what happens later in <u>Act 5</u> can you show you understand how Macbeth is <u>too quick</u> to take their words at <u>face value</u>.

Watch Out For Pretending

Don't forget that occasionally people <u>say</u> things they <u>don't mean</u>. We all do it sometimes and Shakespeare's characters are <u>no different</u>.

Like in Act 2 Scene 3, Macbeth is only <u>pretending</u> to be upset about Duncan — and he's not very good at it. He <u>hams it up</u> a bit. Always remember to think <u>why</u> a character's saying what they say.

Oh, yes, I'm the great pretender...

More than one side to Macbeth — like a coin...

Phew — seems like a lot of <u>complicated stuff</u> to remember. But most of it's <u>common sense</u> really. Get these hints <u>clear</u> in your head and you'll cope fine with this kind of question.

Writing as a Character is HARD

These questions tell you to <u>imagine</u> you're a character in the play and write your answer <u>as if</u> you <u>are</u> that character. Watch it — these babies are <u>much tougher</u> than they look.

It's <u>Not</u> A Simple Game of "<u>Let's Pretend</u>"

It's really tempting to think of these questions as a <u>soft option</u> — like you only have to use your <u>imagination</u>, not look at the play that hard. That's completely <u>wrong</u>.

You've got to do <u>just as much</u> studying the play as for <u>any other</u> question.
And <u>on top</u> of all that you have to <u>remember</u> to pretend you're the character.

That can be <u>pretty difficult</u>. As if you haven't <u>already</u> got enough on your mind in an exam.

> **Act 1 Scene 7, Act 2 Scene 1**
> **Imagine you are Macbeth. Write your diary entry for the day.**

> *First of all I decided not to murder Duncan. Then Lady Macbeth — er, I mean, my dear wife — came in.*
> *When she calls Macbeth a coward, he changes his mind. Sorry, I mean I changed my mind.*

Because you're used to writing normally, as <u>yourself</u>, it's too easy to <u>forget</u> that you're supposed to be Macbeth. Don't fall into this trap — you'll <u>lose marks</u> if you do.

You've Got To Do All The <u>Other Stuff</u> As Well

The other big mistake is forgetting to do all the <u>other stuff</u> I told you in Section 6.

Finished.

Imagine you are Macbeth

Use <u>quotes</u> a lot.
Have a proper <u>plan</u>.
Have a <u>beginning</u>, <u>middle</u> and <u>end</u>.
Show that you <u>understand</u> the scenes.

It's actually a lot <u>harder</u> to do some of this stuff when you're <u>pretending</u> to be a character.

BMWs on TV — that's what I call "car actors"...

Phew — I told you these questions are <u>tough</u>. Beats me why anyone would want to <u>bother</u> with them, frankly. Just make sure you remember that they're <u>not</u> the soft option they seem.

Writing As A Character	# Quotes & Reactions

These pretending-to-be-a-character questions are hard, but <u>not impossible</u>.
Here's how to get the <u>better</u> of them.

You Have to be Careful When Using Quotes

Quoting is one of the things that's <u>tougher</u> when you're imagining you're a character.
The challenge is to make it <u>sound natural</u>.

> I discovered that Duncan had been murdered and rushed to tell the others. "Most sacrilegious Murther hath broke ope the Lord's anointed Temple, and stole thence the life o'th'building!" I told them. Well, you should have seen their faces.

This <u>doesn't</u> sound natural. You wouldn't use <u>great long quotes</u> when you're describing something that <u>happened to you</u>.

This is <u>more like it</u> — it's much easier to make <u>short quotes</u> sound natural.

> We think the guards did it, but we'll never know for sure because Macbeth killed them. I asked him why and he said it was because of his "violent love" for Duncan. I suppose that's fair enough, but I thought it was a bit suspicious.

Say How You React, and What Effect You Have

It's no good only putting a quote down. You have to make it <u>relevant</u> to the story you're telling as a particular character. That means <u>two things</u>:

When you quote something <u>you</u> said, say what <u>effect</u> it had.

A scientist asks: how does Lady Macbeth react to... iodine?

When you quote something <u>someone else</u> said, say how <u>you reacted</u>.

> I was very concerned by my husband's behaviour, so I reminded him his "noble friends" were all present. Thankfully that snapped him out of it and he started to behave normally again, being pleasant and drinking toasts.

> But then he suddenly lost it again, said "quit my sight" to an empty chair and started going on about "marrowless" bones. I was terrified he might say something that gave us away, so once again I had to think quickly.

I'm careful with quoites — oh you said quotes...

Two easy rules: 1) Keep <u>quotes short</u>. 2) Say what <u>effect</u> they had and how people <u>reacted</u>.

How a Character Feels and Thinks

Something else you need to do is write about what your character feels and thinks. You've got to get right under the character's skin and have a good scratch around to see how it feels.

Say What Your Character Feels and Thinks

Sure, you have to say what happens in the scenes you're writing about. But imagining you're a character means you have to imagine what they think and feel about what's happened.

> Act 2 Scene 2, Act 2 Scene 3
> Imagine you are Macbeth. Write down your thoughts and feelings about the events in these scenes.

Saying what happens shows you've read the scenes. But you have to say what Macbeth thinks and feels to show you understand his character — like this:

What are you doing?!

Imagining I'm Macbeth.

> Well, I did it — I killed Duncan. But I felt terrible about it afterwards. I had to get away from the body as quickly as possible, it was so horrible to look at, and in my rush I brought the daggers with me.
>
> My wife told me to take the daggers back but I couldn't bear the thought of going back there, I felt so shaky with nerves and fear. In fact I think my mind might have been playing tricks on me — I thought I heard a voice say "Macbeth doth murther sleep". Maybe it was just my guilty conscience but it really freaked me out.

It's all about striking a balance. On the one hand, you've got to make sure there's evidence in the play for what you say. But on the other, you're allowed to use your imagination to put yourself in the character's place.

> When I walked past the room where Malcolm and Donalbain were, I heard them saying their prayers. I wanted to say "Amen" with them but I couldn't.
>
> This really disturbed me — it was as if I knew God wouldn't approve of what I was doing.

This is straight from the play.

This is using your imagination.

Burnt logs on TV — that's what I call "char-actors"...

It's earth-shatteringly important when you're writing as a character to say what that character thinks and feels about the stuff that's happened. Use your imagination to put yourself in their position.

48

| Writing As A Character | # What They Know & How They Speak |

One last page on imagining you're a character — it's pretty <u>obvious</u> stuff, this, but you'd be amazed at the number of people who get it <u>wrong</u>. Make sure you're not one of them.

Don't Say Things The Character Doesn't Know

Make sure you <u>remember</u> when you're writing as a character that <u>you know more</u> than the character would. Don't <u>slip up</u> and write things the character wouldn't know.

> Look out for things your character <u>wouldn't know</u> because he or she <u>wasn't there</u> at the time.

> *I had to have Banquo killed — he suspects too much. Earlier on today he said I had "play'd most foully" to become King.*

D'oh! Macbeth <u>wouldn't</u> have heard that — Banquo was on the stage <u>alone</u> when he said it.

> And look out for things your character <u>wouldn't know</u> because they <u>haven't happened</u> yet.

> *I've just seen three apparitions. The second one said that "none of woman born" could harm me. I was relieved because it meant I didn't need to fear Macduff. But in my relief I'd forgotten Macduff was born by Caesarean section.*

D'oh! Macbeth <u>doesn't</u> know this when he sees the apparitions in Act 4 — he only finds out <u>later</u>.

Use the Right Kind of Language

<u>NOT</u> the right language.

Like, Macbeth's way cool, I'll make him Thane of Cawder.

Don't forget that when you're writing <u>as a character</u>, you have to try to use the same kind of <u>language</u> that the character would use. In Macbeth, you're pretty certain to be writing as some Scottish <u>nobleman</u> or <u>noblewoman</u>.

Now, that <u>doesn't</u> mean you have to write in <u>11th century</u> Scottish dialect. But it does mean you should sound <u>formal and dignified</u>.

This is how a <u>noble person</u> would write.

This <u>isn't</u>.

> *Our host appeared strangely distracted. I wondered what had caused this sudden change in his behaviour. But his good lady assured us it was nothing to be concerned about.*

> *Macbeth started acting like a nutcase. He'd completely lost it. What on earth was he on?*

Want to measure Lan? — get the right "lan-guage"...

Another page on writing as a character. I said these questions were <u>tough</u>. Remember to use the <u>right</u> kind of <u>language</u>. And you wouldn't say something the <u>character</u> doesn't know... would you?

Section 7 — Types of Questions

Questions About The Mood

This type of question wants you to <u>describe</u> the <u>mood</u> of the scenes you're looking at — and explain <u>how</u> this mood is created.

Say <u>How</u> <u>Shakespeare</u> Creates the Mood

There are <u>a few different tricks</u> Shakespeare uses to create the mood — you've got to <u>spot them</u> and write about them as well as <u>quoting loads</u> and showing you know <u>what's happening</u>. But mentioning them isn't enough, you've got to say <u>how it works</u> as well.

How the Mood is Created
1) Through the <u>language</u>
2) Via <u>stage directions</u>

I'm pig sick of all this rain. Why can't we move somewhere with nice weather like Barbados or Jamaica...

The <u>Witches' language</u> adds to the <u>mood</u> of all their scenes. They talk in strange, short, <u>rhyming</u> sentences. They speak in a <u>different way</u> from all the other characters to <u>set them apart</u> and show that they're <u>magical</u>, <u>supernatural</u> beings.

1 Witch. When shall we three meet again?
          In thunder, lightning, or in rain?
2 Witch. When the hurly-burly's done,
          When the battle's lost and won.
                              Act 1, Scene 1, lines 1-4

[*Thunder. Enter Third Apparition, a child crowned, with a tree in his hand*]
Macbeth   What is this?
                              Act 4, Scene 1, line 85

The <u>thunder</u> in the stage directions here helps create the <u>tense and dramatic</u> mood of the scene.

Translating *the Task Makes it* Easier

Here's a <u>really handy</u> little tip — sometimes this type of question is <u>phrased</u> in a nasty way, but you can <u>always translate</u> them to make them <u>easier to answer</u>. So...

Möchten Sie Tee trinken?

What? Oh, do I want a cuppa? Yeah, go on then, got any biccies?

BECOMES

Describe how Shakespeare makes this scene tense and exciting.

The <u>scene is</u> tense and exciting. <u>Why</u>?

Just try to get rid of <u>scary</u> words like "describe". It'd be the same if the question said "explain", or "say".

Cows like a good atmosphere — the right moo-d...

Moods are <u>darned complicated</u>. You've got to look at all the <u>different factors</u> and cunning ways Shakespeare creates the mood — then write about them all, of course. That'll get you the marks...

How Mood Affects The Audience

There're a few more things to think about as well if you want to get <u>really good marks</u>.

Think About *How the Audience Feels and Why*

Questions like these that ask you about the <u>mood</u> of the scenes don't just want you to talk about the <u>characters</u>, the <u>story</u>, the <u>language</u> and the <u>stage directions</u> — they also want you to talk about <u>how</u> the <u>audience feels</u> and why. Phew... Sounds tricky, but it doesn't have to be.

> Act 3 Scene 4, Act 4 Scene 1
> How does Shakespeare make these scenes frightening?

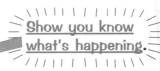
<u>Show you know
what's happening.</u>

<u>Quote loads.</u>

Oh that's
a lovely crown!
Ooh — suit you sir!
Ooh!

Will you stop quoting
that blasted show!

Macbeth is sitting down to a banquet with noble guests when a murderer arrives at the door. Macbeth comments to him, *"There's blood upon thy face"* introducing a sinister air to the scene right at the start. Macbeth hints at his own disturbed state of mind when he hears that only Banquo and not Fleance has been killed,
*"I am cabined, cribbed, confined, bound in
To saucy doubts and fears."*
Shortly after that the stage directions indicate *"[The ghost of Banquo appears and sits in Macbeth's place]"*. The <u>audience knows</u> that Banquo has been murdered and is now on stage as a ghost. We can assume from Macbeth's comment on Banquo's *"gory locks"* that the appearance of the ghost is gruesome. This in itself is <u>frightening</u> and is emphasised by Macbeth's terrified reaction and guiltily insane ravings.

Picking out certain words and writing about their effect is great stuff too.

<u>Mention the effect
of stage directions.</u>

<u>Refer to the task.</u>

> Remember — you still have to show you <u>understand what's happening</u> in the scenes and <u>quote loads</u>. It's mega important for good marks.

Always Think About
<u>All of These</u> if You're
Writing About <u>Mood</u>

1) Characters
2) Story
3) Language
4) Stage Directions
5) The Audience

Eye of frog
And tongue of newt
Dozy cow
Create a mood

MOO-D...

How's an audience feel? — with their fingers...

OK, there's a fair bit to <u>keep in mind</u>, but it's not all that bad. Keep it <u>organised</u> and remember the five different things to write about and that should <u>do the trick</u>. Learn it now to get <u>great marks</u>...

Directing A Scene — The Audience

You might think it's harder to imagine you're a <u>director</u> than imagine you're a character. But here's a <u>nice surprise</u> — when you know what a director does, it's actually loads <u>easier</u>.

You Have to Think About the Audience

The director's job is to help the audience <u>understand</u> and <u>enjoy</u> the play. Shakespeare's <u>tough</u> enough to understand when you've got the <u>words</u> in front of you and your teacher's trying to explain it — so <u>theatre audiences</u> really need the director's <u>help</u> to get what's going on.

Think about it — when you're watching a <u>play</u>, or a film, or something on the telly, you <u>don't</u> need to catch <u>every</u> <u>word</u> to know roughly what's happening. You can usually <u>pick it up</u> from what kind of <u>mood</u> the actors are in, and what <u>tone of voice</u> they say their lines in.

Out, damned spot, out, I say! Hell is murky!

DIRECTOR

Psst... she's supposed to be really unhappy here...

It's the director's job to <u>tell</u> the actors when to <u>shout</u>, when to <u>smile</u>, when to pause and look <u>thoughtful</u>, and so on.

The aim is to help the audience to <u>understand</u> what's happening.

The director also uses other tricks to give the audience <u>clues</u> — like what <u>clothes</u> the characters wear, whether the <u>stage lights</u> are bright or dim, what background <u>sounds</u> there are.

Questions that ask you to direct a scene are <u>great</u> for showing you understand the scene and the language — there are <u>all sorts of things</u> you can write about.

You Still Have to Quote

There's <u>no getting away</u> from it, I'm afraid. Whatever kind of question you do, you're going to need to <u>quote</u> lots, and imagine-you're-a-director questions are <u>no different</u>.

Luckily it's <u>fairly easy</u> to work quotes into these answers.

Quote a bit of the play and then talk about <u>how</u> you want the actors to <u>say the words</u>.

When Macbeth says "Is this a dagger which I see before me", he should be frowning and looking scared and he should say it in a confused, nervous and uncertain way. He should also reach his hand out as if he's trying to touch the dagger.

It's <u>not a problem</u> to work quotes into these answers — just make sure you <u>remember</u> to do it.

Direct to a scene — straight to a tantrum...

Questions that want you to imagine you're a director look <u>tough</u> — but actually they're really <u>cool</u>. They give you <u>loads of opportunity</u> to show you understand what's going on in the scenes.

How The Characters Should Act

The <u>most important</u> thing a director does is tell the actors <u>how to say their lines</u>.
If you get a "director" question, you should write <u>loads</u> about how the lines should be <u>said</u>.

Say How The Actors Should *Say Their Lines*

Imagine how the lines should sound when they're <u>said on stage</u> — and write it down. It's as <u>simple</u> as that. Remember, your task is to <u>help the audience</u> understand the meaning.

Example:
When Macbeth comes on stage after killing Duncan, he should say his lines quietly — the things he's saying are terrifying to him, so he wouldn't want to say them very loud. He should also speak quite quickly because his mind is in turmoil so the words will just be spilling out, without him thinking very hard about them.

Think about whether the lines should be said <u>quietly</u> or <u>loudly</u>, <u>slowly</u> or <u>quickly</u>.

Try to explain <u>why</u> the lines should be said that way.

There's <u>no single right answer</u> to these questions. Often you can interpret scenes in <u>many different ways</u>. So, when he's talking to Banquo's ghost, you could show Macbeth's horror by having him <u>mutter</u> in quiet fear or <u>shout</u> in raging terror. <u>Either</u> would be OK. Look at these examples of how different ways Macbeth could be talking just after he's seen Banquo's ghost:

Example:
Macbeth should sound breezy and self-assured when he says "do not muse at me, my most worthy friends" — he should be making light of his strange behaviour....

Example:
Macbeth should sound really scared when he says "do not muse at me, my most worthy friends" — he should be really unsure like he can't concentrate because of what he just saw.

Different Characters Will *Act Differently*

Don't forget that <u>not all</u> the characters will be acting the <u>same way</u> in a single scene.
A lot of <u>tension</u> comes from different people on stage being in <u>different moods</u>.
Like this:

While Macbeth is mentally falling apart after killing Duncan, Lady Macbeth should be cold, businesslike and in control. Macbeth should be quaking and gibbering when he asks if "all great Neptune's ocean" would wash the blood off his hands. In contrast, Lady Macbeth should be contemptuous of his weakness when she coolly says "a little water clears us of this deed."

Wuss.

Ken Branagh's a "dire actor" — er, I mean "director"...

Ask yourself how the lines should be <u>said</u> — what would the character's mood be at that time, and what <u>tone of voice</u> should they use. And don't forget that <u>different characters</u> act differently.

Appearance & What Characters Do

Telling the actors how to say their lines is only one of the things a director can do.
You should remember all these other handy tricks too if you want to do well on these questions.

Tell the Actors What To Do

It's not just what they say that counts — they can communicate a lot by body language.
Tell them how to carry out the stage directions. Like in Act 2 Scene 2 when Macbeth enters,
you could tell him to walk on slowly, looking in dazed disbelief at the bloody daggers in his hand.

You can use your imagination too — this stuff isn't in the stage directions, but it's great because it helps the audience to grasp what's going on.

When Macbeth first sees Banquo's ghost, he should jump to show he's startled and take a step back in fear. Before Lady Macbeth says "Are you a man?", she should grab Macbeth firmly by the arm and march him off into a corner so the other guests can't hear what they're saying.

Lighting and Sound can Create a Mood

Sometimes the stage directions tell you what kind of sounds there should be. In Act 1,
at the start of both Scene 1 and Scene 3 the stage direction says "Thunder". And at the
end of Act 2 Scene 3 the stage direction tells you there should be a knocking sound.

The aim of these sounds is to make the audience feel in a mood that suits the scene.
If you have ideas of your own, stick them in too — you could have the sound of
wind howling through trees in Act 1 Scene 3, adding to the eerie, scary feeling.

As director you can control the lighting, too — and again your aim is to create an
appropriate mood. Nasty things seem even scarier in the dark — so you could have
Macbeth's castle very dark and lit only by candles in the first two scenes of Act 2.

Put them in the Right Clothes

You can also help the audience to understand things by
making sure the clothes are appropriate.

For example, you could have Duncan dressed in gold and
white to show he's royal and good. Or give the Witches
pointy hats and black capes to show they're witches.

Or you could have Macduff dressed in an impressive suit of
armour in Act 5, to show what a great soldier he is.

Hmm... maybe not.

20000V in Act 3 — I said lighting, not lightning...

Directors can do tons of things to help audiences get a feel for what's happening — they can
decide on clothes, say what the sound and lighting should be, and tell the actors what to do.

Writing As A Director	# Directing — The Mood

I've already talked about how you can use <u>sound and lighting</u> to create a <u>mood</u>. Well, you can do the same thing with the <u>words</u> too. It all depends on <u>how</u> you tell the actors to say them.

The <u>Words</u> can Also Create a <u>Mood</u>

You know from page 49 how Shakespeare uses <u>language</u> to create a mood. You can write the <u>same stuff</u> in writing-as-a-director questions. Only this time you talk <u>not just</u> about the words, but about how you want the actors to <u>say</u> them.

Audiences don't just want to <u>understand</u> the play — they also want to be <u>moved</u> by it. It's <u>your job</u> as director to make the scary bits seem scary, the sad bits seem sad, and so on — that's what <u>creating a mood</u> is all about.

When the Witches talk to Macbeth and Banquo, they should speak in a screechy, cackling way. They look horrible so their voices should sound horrible too. This will make the mood of the scene even more creepy and frightening.

When they talk in riddles to Banquo — "Lesser than Macbeth, and greater" — they should say the words in a mysterious way, as if they know more than they're letting on, as if they're teasing him. This will make the audience feel even more impressed with their supernatural knowledge.

The Mood can <u>Change</u> Within a Scene

Often the audience feels <u>different things</u> at <u>different times</u> in a scene.
How you tell the actors to <u>say their lines</u> can really <u>help</u> the audience to feel these different moods.

Macduff should say the words "untimely ripp'd" with a great dramatic flourish. This is a revelation both to Macbeth and to the audience and so it is a very exciting moment.

Then the mood of the scene should change as Macbeth says his next speech in a quiet, shaken way — he should sound like a broken man as he says "I'll not fight with thee".

Then when Macbeth does decide to fight, he should say "Yet I will try to the last" with great dignity and courage. He should be reminding the audience what a brave and great warrior he is, and what a tragedy it is that he did such evil things.

In Act 5 Scene 8 the mood <u>changes quickly</u>. It's <u>exciting</u> when Macduff and Macbeth fight, then there's the <u>shock</u> of Macduff's revelation. Then finally the mood is <u>tragic</u> as Macbeth is going to die.

This play's like a removals van — really moving...

When you're writing as a <u>director</u>, remember the director can help create the <u>mood</u> of a scene by telling the actors how to say their lines. You want the play to affect how the audience <u>feel</u>.

Revision Summary

Yes, you're nearly there — it's the last page of the book. But don't put it down and get the video game out just yet. You still have to make sure you know everything in this section. And I mean everything. It's a really important section — after all, the whole point of this book is to help you do better in your SAT, and this section gives you loads of handy advice on the specific types of question they're going to ask you. So make sure you know this stuff well enough to answer these revision questions in your sleep.

1) What are the three key steps for success?

2) The major characters in Macbeth have more than one side to them. True or false?

3) Is it only what the characters say that counts, or what they do as well?

4) Why does it help to know what happens in the rest of the play?

5) Do characters sometimes say things they don't mean?

6) If you get an "imagine you're a character" question, is it likely to be:
   (a) a piece of cake, or   *(b)* a tough cookie?

7) On these "imagine you're a character" questions, do you still have to bother with all that stuff from Section Six?

8) Is it easier to make short or long quotes sound natural when you're writing as a character?

9) What two things help to make a quote relevant when you're writing as a character?

10) Should you just say what happened, or should you say what your character thought and felt about it as well?

11) Can you use your imagination?

12) You should make sure you don't say things in "writing as a character" questions that your character wouldn't know: what are the two main ways this could happen?

13) When writing as a character, is using the right kind of language:
   (a) very very important,   or   *(b)* not that important really?

14) What are two major ways that Shakespeare creates a mood?

15) When the question asks about the mood of some scenes, it's important you imagine how the audience would feel and react to it. True or false?

16) Which of these things does a director do?
   (a) tells the actors how to say their lines.
   (b) gets the actors a nice cup of tea and a slice of carrot cake.
   (c) tells the actors when and how to move about the stage.
   (d) reads the narrator's parts.
   (e) decides what clothes the actors wear.
   (f) decides what sounds there are.
   (g) decides how the stage is lit.

17) Is there only one correct way the lines should be said?

I hate these typing questions...

NO! *Types* of questions!

Index

Index

The Six Big Shakespeare Blunders

Loads of people go horribly wrong with Shakespeare in the SAT because they keep making these SIX BIG BLUNDERS. Don't be one of the clowns who makes a complete hash of it on the big day.

THE SIX BIG HORRIBLE "NO-NO"s

1) NOT FOLLOWING THE INSTRUCTIONS

If you don't follow the instructions, you'll do the wrong thing and get no marks.

2) NOT READING THE WHOLE SCENE

Don't skip bits just because you think they're boring — you'll miss something important.

3) NOT DOING ALL THE BITS THEY ASK YOU TO

If you only do half of the task, you'll only get half the marks.

4) NOT DOING MORE THAN JUST RE-TELLING THE STORY

Do exactly what the task says. Re-telling the story isn't going to be enough — you have to write about other things like the language and how it looks on stage.

5) NOT QUOTING PROPERLY

Always give quotes to back up your answer — but don't quote great long chunks — a couple of lines is much, much better.

6) NOT WRITING PROPERLY

— you must write in nice paragraphs.
— and write in a <u>nice style</u> too, with plenty of interesting words.
— proper spelling and proper grammar please.
— always <u>check it</u> once you've written it.

Don't be a clown...
learn your stuff — and get it right